M000191681

World Record Whitetail: The Hanson Buck Story
By *Milo Hanson* as told to *Ian McMurchy*

Published by

krause publications

700 E. State Street • Iola, WI 54990-0001

Please call or write for our free catalog of outdoor publications. Our toll-free number to place an order or obtain a free catalog is 800-258-0929, or please use our regular business telephone, 715-445-2214, for editorial comment or further information.

Library of Congress Catalog Number: 95-77305
ISBN: 0-87341-363-6
Printed in the United States of America

Dedication

This book is dedicated to Olive Hanson: my wife, my partner, and my hunting companion.

And to Bradley, Chris and Walter. Thanks boys.

Acknowledgements

On Nov., 23, 1993, the Hanson Buck forever changed my life. Since that day, many people have shared my appreciation of this great buck. I would like to acknowledge some special people who have helped and supported me.

First, my hunting partners: Walter Meger, Rene Igini and John Yaroshko. What a deer hunt we had that day! These fellows know how to hunt and they all contributed to my success. I will always be grateful.

Ian McMurchy is a well-known wildlife photographer. Ian's advice, guidance and friendship have made the dealings with the Hanson Buck much easier. Thank you, Ian.

Everyone agrees that the Hanson Buck display does complete justice to the majesty of this great buck. For that I am grateful to Bub Hill, the master taxidermist from the little town of Briercrest, Saskatchewan, Canada.

I wish to thank the Biggar Wildlife Federation for the wonderful support and assistance that has been, and continues to be, provided to me and my family. I also thank all the people of Biggar and the region — rural and towns — for showing such interest in me and the Hanson Buck.

Finally, I must say that I can't possibly thank everyone who has entered my life since I shot the Hanson Buck, but I assure all of you that I treasure your kindness and good wishes.

— *Milo Hanson, June 1995*

Table of Contents

Introduction

Milo Hanson, 49, a Saskatchewan farmer, made white-tailed deer hunting history Nov. 23, 1993, when he shot a buck carrying the largest typical antlers ever scored by the Boone and Crockett Club. The Hanson Buck goes into the record book with a score of 213-5/8 inches, replacing the 206-1/8 Jordan Buck of Wisconsin, which was shot in 1914.

Milo shot his great buck on his own land, located several miles north of Biggar, a small town in west-central Saskatchewan. Milo and three close friends — Walter Meger, Rene Igini and John Yaroshko — hunted hard for the huge buck. After several missed opportunities over several days, the world's largest buck became the Hanson Buck when Milo's .308 bullets brought him down. At that moment, even though he did not yet know it, Milo Hanson had realized every deer hunter's dream: to get the world's biggest buck.

I was fortunate and grateful to be asked by Milo and his wife, Olive, to do the official photography of the Hanson Buck. Even more important to me is the fact that the Hansons and I have become good friends, and are sharing some great times.

As you will see, Milo and Olive have had their lives changed by this great buck. I hope you enjoy their story.

Chapter 1

Milo Hanson: Farmer and Hunter

I was born in 1945 in southwestern Saskatchewan. In fact, my father and brother still ranch and farm near the town of Eastend. My father, E.O. Hanson, who recently turned 80, lives on one of the ranches about 15 miles from Eastend. I was named after my mother's brother, who was killed in World War II shortly before my birth. My wife, Olive, grew up in the Biggar, Saskatchewan, area, where her family first homesteaded in 1928.

Everyone in my family hunted. Like most prairie kids, I grew up hunting varmints, game birds and eventually, big game. Because southwestern Saskatchewan has a tremendous variety of wildlife, we all learned to appreciate nature and the outdoors.

I began hunting big game with my father when I was about

*Milo Hanson's farm is located near Biggar, and his father still
ranches and farms near the town of Eastend, Saskatchewan.
Here, Hanson's brother David, left, his father, E. O. Hanson,
center, and Hanson pose by Milo's world record buck.*

15. We hunted mule deer, antelope and whitetails. I shot my
first big-game animal, a white-tailed doe, when I was 15.
Back then, everyone used a Lee Enfield .303 British, or the
cowboy's favorite, the Model 94 in .30-30 Winchester.

Between the ages of 14 and 17, I worked for ranchers
around Eastend, putting up hay and feeding cattle. After
high school, I worked on oil rigs in the Shaunavon area. Our
crew had the dirty job in the oil patch: We serviced oil
pumps, which made us grimy and oil-saturated every day. In
the mid-1960s, I took a job in the co-op lumber yard in the
town of Shaunavon.

Olive moved into the area about this time. We met in 1964
and were married within a year. Olive's father died in 1969,

Milo and Olive Hanson grow grain crops and raise about 100 cows on their Biggar-area farm.

and we were offered the chance to operate her family's farm in the Biggar area. We took over a beef cattle operation on 1,200 acres, of which about 200 acres were suitable for cropping. The rest was pasture and bush.

Cattle prices declined in the late 1970s, and we had to change the farming operation to remain viable. We converted to grain production, which necessitated breaking up much of our pasture land. I purchased a bulldozer and spent hundreds of hours knocking down trees and clearing brush to make more fields, both for us and neighboring farmers. We have been growing more grain crops than ever, mostly wheat, oats and barley. In addition, cattle prices have been good in recent years, so we raise about 100 bred cows on our pasture or on rented pastures nearby. Today we operate a mixed farm comprised of cultivated land and 1,300 acres of pas-

Milo's son Bradley, left, was born in 1970. He returns home regularly to work on the family farm.

ture.

Olive gave birth to our son, Bradley, in 1970. In 1982, Olive and I took another young man into our family, initially as a hired hand, and gradually he became our unofficial adopted son. Chris is a little older than Bradley, and he considers our home to be his. Brad and Chris have worked together in the oil fields in Alberta, and they return home to work on the farm, particularly at harvest time. Bradley is becoming more involved with farming and will soon make it his career.

Harvest requires lots of manpower and long hours. Everyone in the family operates swathers, combines and grain trucks. After harvest we put away the swathers and combines, pick a few rocks and do a little field preparation. We then prepare for the hunting seasons, which are a special

Milo bought his lever-action Winchester Model 88 .308 in 1970. He was using this rifle when he shot the world-record white-tailed buck.

holiday for our family and friends.

An important part of my hunting life occurred in 1970 when I bought a Winchester Model 88 lever-action rifle in .308 Winchester. That old rifle has served me well ever since. I bought it new at the hardware store in Biggar, complete with a Weaver K-4 scope mounted in Weaver rings. The whole rig cost $189, which in those days was a lot of money for a rifle. When hunting, I carry an extra clip with four 150-grain cartridges. The Model 88 and the Weaver scope have bounced around in vehicles for many years, but have always remained accurate. Besides hunting for deer, antelope, elk and moose, I carry the "88" to shoot coyotes around the farm.

I feel fortunate to be married to Olive. Besides being a

Milo's wife, Olive, is a skilled farmer, gardener, cook and big-game hunter.

skilled farmer, gardener and fantastic cook, she is a hunter. She started hunting as a young girl, pursuing small game and game birds with her brothers. She didn't deer hunt until after our marriage, when she realized it would allow us to spend more time together.

Olive killed her first buck with a long shot, which greatly impressed me. She stopped hunting for a while after Brad's birth in 1970. She resumed hunting in about 1980, mostly going with me and our friends. Olive occasionally hunts on her own, but only on our land. A few years ago she shot a buck while on a solo hunt, and then went hunting for me. I was hunting nearby with friends. After she found me, she dragged me over to her buck to field-dress it!

Olive hunts with a Remington 760 pump in .243 Winchester. The rifle's stock is a bit long for her, but she shoots it well enough and prefers not to change it. Besides, Brad likes to borrow her rifle at times, so we can't shorten the stock or it wouldn't fit him. There have been tense days when Brad is home and wants to go hunting on the same day his mom planned to hunt. Olive always gives in and lets Brad use the rifle.

Each autumn we take three or four weeks and hunt white-tails, antelope, mule deer, moose and sometimes elk. Olive doesn't usually go on hunts where travel is required, such as for antelope, moose or elk. She prefers to hunt near home for whitetails and muleys.

Almost everyone in our area hunts and, for some reason, our farm — and my shop, in particular — seems to be the gathering point. Maybe this is because it's heated, and equipped for hanging and skinning deer.

Each hunting day varies as neighbors show up to plan a hunt. I hunt regularly with several close friends. Still, other friends hunt with us when they find time.

We all enjoy trying to get the biggest buck in the area, but none of us is a serious trophy hunter. Our local wildlife federation club has a big-buck contest, and while we all want to win the trophy, that's the extent of our interest in trophy whitetails and how they're scored. Because the club has always had one or two guys who knew how to score, I never learned much about the Boone and Crockett Club's system until shooting the Hanson Buck. We would get our racks scored at the Buck Night supper, and never worried about the intricacies of net and gross scores for typical and non-typical racks. In fact, I didn't know the B&C Club maintained such a detailed record book, or that being in the book could mean so much to some hunters.

I am fortunate to live in a region that has some huge bucks, but they seldom come easy. I have shot some big bucks over the years, and most of the racks ended up on the wall in my shop. However, one buck that scored 147 is mounted and hangs above our mantle.

Quite simply, while big racks intrigue me, the hunt itself has always been more important.

Chapter 2

The Home of
the Hanson Buck

Biggar, Saskatchewan, is home to about 2,600 people. Visitors always enjoy our town's motto: "New York is big, but this is Biggar," which is found on signs along the highway and on buildings.

Biggar has always been associated with the Canadian National Railroad. Train crews live here because Biggar is a switching point for the numerous freight trains that travel the province. Like many small towns on the prairies, Biggar is fighting to stay alive, and its survival depends on agriculture. The success of the area's farms determines the town's health. A large malt plant was recently built, which has provided many jobs. This addition has helped Biggar hold its own.

The Biggar region had few, if any, deer when the first European settlers arrived in the early 1900s. Elk still roamed

15

Much of the countryside around Milo Hanson's farm is rolling farmland mixed with aspens and willows.

the prairies, but there were few trees and woods to attract and hold whitetails. Old-timers say they had to travel 20 miles north just to cut firewood for the winter. In those days they also used horse-drawn wagons or sleighs to travel north in search of deer and moose. One of my neighbors, Jack Allen, recalls that 1931 was the first time he saw deer on his land. During those early decades of the 1900s, trees and brush slowly invaded the prairie, and more wildlife moved in. Some old-timers and researchers believe unchecked prairie fires kept trees from taking hold before this century, and as agriculture took over, the trees took off.

The countryside around our place is rolling farmland. About one-third of the area is aspen and willows, particularly in the lower lands. Most of the fields now produce crops, although a few pastures remain. Our farm's soil is classed as a sandy loam and is of average fertility. Many of the grain fields cover 160 acres, and most contain a few scattered aspen bluffs. Almost every field is surrounded by a three-strand barbwire fence because we frequently put cattle onto the stubble in late autumn after harvest. We don't have a major river or lake in our area, so deer water at sloughs or man-made dugouts.

Our plantings provide a lot of quality food for whitetails. In recent years, canola has been in strong demand. Many fields that traditionally grew grains now grow canola. In addition, wheat, barley and oats remain common, and many farmers have planted field peas and lentils because these crops are also in demand. Some years our wheat yields as much as 30 to 35 bushels per acre. We also grow alfalfa for our cattle's winter feed.

The climate around Biggar is typical of northern prairies, with hot and cold extremes that make many people wonder why anyone willingly lives in Saskatchewan. Summer highs soar into the 90s, and winter lows plummet into the minus 40s. Some winters we get 2 or 3 feet of snow, particularly in the bluffs. Our area receives decent rainfall, averaging 12 inches per year. Summer 1993 was extraordinary because we received more than 17 inches of rain. I've speculated that the abundant moisture that year might have contributed to the growth of my buck's antlers because the browse and vegetation were in excellent condition.

Most of my neighbors agree the white-tailed deer population has increased in our area since the 1970s. Part of this might be that the switch from raising cattle to producing grain has allowed aspen bluffs and willow runs to return. This underbrush provides natural browse and dense cover for whitetails. When driving at night, we must now be careful because of abundant deer. Almost everyone we know has hit a deer with their vehicle. Olive and I have had a couple of bad collisions with deer, including one only a few weeks after we bought a new pickup.

The Biggar region grows big white-tailed bucks, but I don't think anyone can claim it's the province's top overall producer. I know of a big 170-class buck killed about one mile from our house several years ago. But until shooting the Hanson Buck, I thought the buck hanging over the mantel in my home, which scored 147, was a great buck. That might be because our region has long produced a good number of

The Biggar, Sask. region has long produced good numbers of bucks in the 135- to 150-class range. The Saskatchewan Wildlife Federation lists 184 bucks that score more than 175 points.

bucks in the 135- to 150-class range, and it continued to produce a number of excellent bucks in 1994. In fact, I shot a buck in November 1994 that scored in the 170s.

As an aside, until shooting the Hanson Buck and becoming more familiar with the Boone & Crockett scoring system, we typically classified our bucks based on the "Western" count. For instance, we first referred to the Hanson Buck as a "6-point," not a "12-point," as it's called by Eastern hunters. Of course, still other hunters prefer to use the more descriptive method, describing it as a "6-by-6." I guess I prefer this last description.

Hunting season in the Biggar area is a time of relaxation and enjoyment. Olive and I have always looked forward to the late autumn so we can get out with friends and neighbors. These outings also include a lot of scouting and planning before the season opens. Deer hunting becomes the main topic in our lives when the season finally arrives.

While everyone in our group can become competitive about deer hunting, it has always been a friendly rivalry, not something to inspire jealousy or boastfulness. Further, we never paid much attention to which big bucks dominate the Boone and Crockett Club's record book. In fact, I never realized the importance many people place on deer antlers, and that some heads become legendary. Maybe I wasn't aware of that phenomenon because of Saskatchewan's history with B&C bucks. While our province has many bucks in the record books, until now, none placed high enough to become as notable as the "Hole in the Horn" buck or the Jordan Buck.

Also, our province has its own record book. The Saskatchewan Wildlife Federation compiles provincial big-game scores in the Henry Kelsey record book. The book's 1992 edition lists 184 bucks that score more than 175 points. Until my entry, the province's record typical whitetail was a 204-6/8 buck taken by Peter Swistun of Mayfair, Saskatchewan, in 1983. In 1992, Bruce Ewen of Archerwill shot a 203-7/8 buck. Of the top five bucks in the 1992 edition, three were taken in the 1990s, one in the 1980s and one in the 1970s.

The big-game hunting zone around Biggar, however, is restricted to Saskatchewan and Canadian residents only. Hunters from the United States can hunt upland birds and waterfowl here, but they must travel north a few hours to the provincial-forest zones to hunt whitetails. The province has studied proposals to allow Americans to hunt the province's agricultural areas, but at least through 1995, the idea has never been implemented. Still, the forest zones are known to produce excellent deer, and many outfitters specialize in guiding deer hunts up there. I have met some of these outfitters, and I've been impressed with the services they provide. I've also been impressed by the bucks their clients shoot.

Of course, be aware that some hunting techniques might differ from how you hunt near home. For example, baiting deer is legal in Saskatchewan. Most outfitters use grain or alfalfa to attract deer to an area, and hunters sit in tree stands or tower blinds to watch for bucks. Many outfitters even offer heated blinds so a hunter can sit a long time in cold, severe weather. Good outfitters also rely on rattling, grunting and decoys to coax a buck past their clients. Guided hunts for Saskatchewan's whitetails have become a big business, and everyone says the Hanson Buck greatly increased the demand for those services.

If you're interested in a Saskatchewan hunt, plan ahead. Good outfitters are booked one or two years in advance. For more information write to these sources:

Saskatchewan Outdoor Adventure
Tourism Saskatchewan
500 - 1900 Albert St.
Regina, Saskatchewan, Canada S4P 4L9;

Saskatchewan Outfitters Association
Box 2016
Prince Albert, Saskatchewan, Canada S6V 6K1

Chapter 3

The Hanson Buck's History

"Milo, there's a baby elk out by your place!"

Those words still ring clear as I recall the first time I heard about the deer destined to be known as the Hanson Buck. Jim Angelopoulos, the area's school bus driver, spoke those words one morning as we drank coffee.

Jim raises beef cattle, and his farm lies at the edge of Biggar. He has driven the bus more than 12 years, providing daily transportation during the school year for about 25 local youngsters. Jim hunted deer earlier in his life, but now prefers to simply watch wildlife. And driving a bus in the Biggar area provides plenty of such opportunities. He has seen everything from moose to antelope while traveling his 50-mile route.

Typically, Jim takes the same route to school every morning to ensure he gets the students to class on time. In the

21

Although Milo Hanson never saw his world-record buck before 1993, two neighbors told him about their sightings of the massive deer.

afternoon, however, the bus route can vary because time isn't always a constraint. He has found that students enjoy varying the afternoon route a bit, which allows Jim to sometimes take back routes to watch for wildlife. He doesn't go out of his way, but a good system of roads north of Biggar provides a few travel options.

Generally speaking, the bus trips occur during prime time periods for seeing wildlife, which is early morning and late afternoon. Jim leaves his home about 7:30 a.m., and returns about 5 p.m. Because the bus travels the same route each morning, Jim is certain the deer are used to its presence. Typically, deer show no fear and frequently don't even look up as they feed in the vast fields around Biggar.

Driving the bus has also made Jim more knowledgeable about wildlife. For instance, he has learned much about where the animals and birds are typically found. He also knows their feeding habits and habitat preferences. He and the students have become proficient at spotting wildlife, and they point out birds and animals as the bus moves along.

Jim first saw the big buck in 1992. Initially, he thought the buck was a mule deer because its rack was so wide and tall.

"I saw the buck several times, and he appeared to have a rocking chair on his head," Jim said. "I started watching for him as we traveled through his home range. He was fairly easy to distinguish because his body was not that big, but his antlers were enormous. He was not a spooky animal. Maybe he got used to seeing the bus at the same time of day. I usually saw him alone."

Jim wishes he could have just once seen the buck when its antlers were in velvet, but it never happened. That's probably because the school year ended while the buck's rack was regrowing, and the new school year began after its velvet was shed.

Jim will never forget opening day of the 1992 deer season. That morning he was following a pickup truck occupied by two deer hunters. As the bus approached a large, dry slough, Jim saw the huge buck standing broadside to the road at about 100 yards. The truck ahead just kept going without slowing down. Obviously, its occupants didn't see the buck.

Jim then noticed another truck with deer hunters was behind the bus. He watched in the bus's mirrors as they, too, drove by the huge buck. The buck never moved as the three vehicles proceeded past. Jim thinks the occupants of both trucks were likely distracted by his school bus.

"If they only knew what they had missed!" he said.

Jim saw the buck one other time that year. On that day, the big-racked deer was following a buck that was hot on the trail of a doe. The big-antlered buck acted cautious, however, and did not aggressively try to move in.

During autumn 1993, Jim saw the big buck several times. Jim was alone in the bus one morning when he spotted the buck grazing in a small patch of alfalfa. He stopped his bus and opened its front door so he could get a better look at the monster. The buck continued to graze without a care, so Jim slowly got down from the bus and stood watching from outside its door. The buck looked right back at him but didn't leave. All the while, Jim was wishing he had brought a camera.

On two other occasions, he saw the buck at close range. One of those sightings occurred at about 25 or 30 yards as the buck fed near the road.

Since the buck was killed, many local hunters have asked Jim if he has seen other big bucks in the area. He has even had requests to take a hunter along to watch as he drives his routes, but he declines, stating he isn't a guide. When reflecting on all the deer he has seen over the years, Jim says he has seen lots of bucks, but he might never again see one as large as the Hanson Buck.

"I'm pleased to be able to say that I watched the world-record buck when he was alive," Jim said. "No one could know that he would become the world record, especially Milo. That buck was a beautiful sight."

Although I never saw the buck before the 1993 hunting season, I had heard about it from my neighbor, John Kowalchuk. He had seen a huge buck in velvet near his home, and he had seen a similar buck feeding in nearby fields. He was sure it was the same deer. John described the buck as a 6-by-6 whose rack was wide and tall. He believed the buck was hanging out in some pastures because he saw it as he checked his cows.

Needless to say, when I heard John's descriptions, I became very interested in hunting this big buck. He sounded like an exceptional trophy.

Chapter 4

Our Deer Hunting Method

Like many Saskatchewan deer hunters, our group cruises the roads and trails early each morning in 4x4 pickup trucks. We look for animals that are still feeding in fields or returning to cover from feeding.

Even when I'm not hunting, I find early morning to be one of my favorite times of the day. The wildlife is active, and I enjoy the fantastic sunrises that can only be seen from the prairies. Beyond that, the first hour of each day is always full of anticipation because you never know when you'll see deer.

Everyone has favorite areas they like to check at first light. We park on knolls and hilltops, scan the area with binoculars, and then slowly move on. Besides looking for animals, we carefully check fresh tracks in the snow.

After the first couple of hours, we meet to discuss what we've seen. We also plan our next step, which usually involves "pushing bush." This simply means that we post some hunters on stand while the rest of us walk through woodlots and aspen bluffs, trying to push deer past the standers. We sometimes combine with other hunting parties to do big drives. We push bush and follow deer through the snow until everyone gets too cold or tired. Then we take a break, build a good fire, and warm up and relax for a while. This midday routine has become a tradition with our hunting group. We like building the fire each day because, besides its warmth, the fire allows us to roast sausage and bacon, which make for a hearty meal. We wash it all down with lots of coffee.

Why do we cruise at dawn and dusk, and conduct drives in between? A primary reason is the prairie's cold weather. The Saskatchewan rifle season is held in November and early December. We expect lots of snow and bitter cold temperatures. The temperatures occasionally drop to minus 30 degrees and more. A human being cannot stand around long in those temperatures, especially when the wind is blowing. Everyone takes turns pushing bush and standing. Alternating the duties allows us to share the shooting opportunities when we're standing, and a chance to warm up when "pushing" and burning calories. The pushers occasionally get some shooting, but usually they only hear the shots and the stories about how many deer ran out ahead of them.

Unlike stand hunting, where the deer are sometimes never aware of the hunter's presence, our method rarely provides shots at standing or walking deer. Our shooting opportunities occur as the driven animals break from cover and race across large, open expanses of field or countryside. Sometimes that means we take long shots at running deer. Hunters who are inexperienced at this type of shooting often get frustrated because there is little time to think about the shots.

Some hunters up here practice shooting at moving targets by rolling old car tires down a hill, or shooting at balloons blown by the wind. Hunting coyotes also provides good practice because we usually shoot at them as they run.

Still, I've found there is only one way to learn to hit running deer, and that is through repetition. We keep trying until we learn how far to lead them. This requires that we hunt a lot and learn from our misses.

Most hunters in our area carry fast-operating rifles such as pump-actions. Clip-fed rifles are also an advantage because we frequently must reload in a hurry. All of us use scopes because the shots we take often exceed 200 yards, and open sights don't provide proper aiming at such distances.

Now, I realize some American hunters might find such shooting contrary to everything they've been taught about deer hunting. All I can say is that the terrain and wide-open spaces in which we hunt are far different from what most deer hunters will ever experience. Therefore, before viewing our method harshly, I ask that you consider the challenges our unique habitat presents.

At this point, let me explain a few other important aspects of our style of hunting. For one, we need snow for tracking. We rely on fresh snowfalls to cover up old sign and provide evidence of recent deer movements. In addition, snow allows us to spot deer more easily in the fields and against snow-filled aspen bluffs. It also allows us to follow deer for considerable distances, which played a large role in our hunt for the Hanson Buck.

We also consider the wind when setting up a push because we've found the deer in our area prefer to move into the wind. While it's important to position the standers and "point men" where they have a good field of view, we also take care to ensure the wind won't carry their scent to the deer.

Over the years we've learned where deer usually move after they've been pushed or shot at. Deer, of course, are creatures of habit and I believe they teach their young the best escape routes. In most cases these routes take advantage of low-lying terrain, and they're frequently the shortest distances between two patches of cover. We have also found that bucks tend to use certain areas year after year. We've even named a few spots, such as "Buck Slough." But the bigger white-tailed bucks can be unpredictable, and so we occasionally check areas that have not been hunted much.

Another factor we consider is the crops on area farms. It's important to know what each field contains, especially after snow covers them. Deer prefer some stubble, or rye and alfalfa fields in late fall and winter until the snow becomes too deep. In addition, deer always seem to locate grain piles and any unharvested crop that has been left out. We closely watch these areas.

We get around during hunting season with 4X4 pickups, two guys to a truck. Everyone in our area gets along fairly well, and we hunt with a variety of individuals. The area we hunt is huge, and we must always consider access because some roads quickly blow shut with snow. We also must know the location of gates in the many fields we hunt. Knowing these locations allows us to easily move from one spot to another without going the long way by road.

We don't have to worry about trespassing because most of the land we hunt is owned by someone in our group. Still, some of the neighbors post their fields, in which case we set up our drives to move deer away from the posted land.

Chapter 5

My Hunting Partners

The three fellows who were with me when I shot the Hanson Buck are not only old friends, they're good hunters. Walter Meger works at a large feed lot near Biggar, and Rene Igini and John Yaroshko are neighboring farmers.

Walter, 42, visits our farm almost daily to help out or work in the shop. He started deer hunting in 1970 with a sporterized .303 Lee Enfield army rifle, like just about every hunter in Saskatchewan. He now hunts mainly with a Remington 760 pump in .270 caliber, but he is deadly with a wide variety of guns. He keeps in form by hunting coyotes each winter with a .22-250, shooting most of them on the run.

Walter is a serious hunting addict. He loves scouting for deer and he watches for bucks year-round. During deer season, he gets us up hours before hunting time each morning for a big breakfast and lots of coffee. Walter is also skilled at

Milo hunts the Biggar area with several close friends. When he isn't hunting with his group, Milo often hunts by himself. Lately, he has taken up rattling to attract big bucks.

spotting game, and knows our area well. He often predicts where deer will most likely feed and move. Walter has an impressive collection of more than 20 white-tailed deer racks in his basement. His best buck would score in the 155 to 160 range, but he is not too enthusiastic about scoring the racks. Score sheets aren't important to him. He just loves hunting deer. Besides deer, Walter has also taken moose, mule deer and antelope over the years.

Milo and his hunting partners have taken many white-tailed deer, mule deer, elk and antelope. Some of their racks are displayed in Milo's shed.

Rene is of Swiss descent, and he farms three miles west of our place. He started hunting when he was 18, and shot his first deer in 1961. He has now hunted almost 35 years, and has accumulated a fascinating collection of hunting licenses. I think he has kept virtually every license he ever bought, and most of them were filled, including ones for deer, elk, moose and antelope. We have hunted together since Olive and I moved to the farm.

John is of Ukrainian descent, and he and his wife run a farm 2.5 miles northeast of our home. He started hunting in 1948. Back then, deer were scarce and a deer license entitled you to shoot anything you saw, whitetail or muley. His first gun was a .303 Savage, and he used it to hunt deer, elk and moose. We have been close friends since we started farming, and we have always hunted together. John is an expert marksman, whether he's shooting .22s or big-caliber rifles. For more than 20 years he hunted with an army surplus .303 that didn't have a rear sight. He became so good at shooting without a rear sight that he never replaced it!

John now shoots a Tikka in .30-06 Springfield and a Savage 99 in .308 Winchester. He shoots coyotes around his farm, not only for practice but to reduce the number of predators. He's also a great moose hunter who loves the bush country. Among the big animals he's taken is an enormous moose whose 50-inch rack is mounted in his shop.

Most of the fellows in our group shoot Federal or Winchester factory ammunition in their rifles. Walter and I obtained a reloading outfit, and he makes ammo for some of our rifles. He prefers to use handloads. He enjoys watching for good deals on ammo, and usually picks up enough to keep us going.

We hunt well together as a group, and share information on the deer we see throughout the year. And because three of us farm the areas we hunt, and Walter continually drives and scouts this land, we stay on top of the deer in our area.

Chapter 6

The Fateful Hunting Season: Week 1

When deer season opened Nov. 15, 1993, everyone in our group was looking forward to a few weeks of deer hunting. We had sighted in our rifles and spent time practicing shooting. In addition, we had logged a lot of scouting hours and spotted many deer.

Walter Meger, especially, had covered a lot of ground. Every time he visited our farm, he took a different route so he could check particular fields and cover. It seemed everyone was talking about deer hunting that autumn. The word was out that a huge buck had been seen in our area.

Our usual procedure every hunting season is to make a few phone calls to see what the other guys are doing, and then set up a hunt for the next day or two. Our group can change daily because some of the fellows frequently have other commitments, or they're away on moose or elk hunts.

Milo and several friends saw some nice bucks during the first week of the 1993 firearms season. However, they decided to wait for a larger deer — preferably the "huge guy" they knew was in the area.

Olive, Walter and I often hunt together, usually with one or two other hunters. We tend to limit the groups to four or five hunters. We usually meet at my home or shop about 8:30 a.m., and split up in pairs to cruise for an hour or two. We always arrange to meet at a certain time and location to plan the pushes.

Like everyone around us in November 1993, Olive and I were excited about the coming deer season. But when the big day came, Nov. 15, we had to attend a funeral, and could only hunt for a while in the morning.

We saw several deer, but nothing of any size while hunting. Predictably enough, late in the day we saw two decent bucks while driving home from the funeral!

Hunting was tough the first few days because no new snow had fallen. We found deer tracks everywhere, but it was difficult to separate the fresh from the old. Still, the weather was comfortable. The temperatures hovered around freezing, so we could push the bush without having to stop to warm up.

On the season's first day, Dwayne Zagoruy, a young neighbor of ours, walked into an area where his sister had recently seen the big buck. Dwayne saw the buck, but it went into some heavy cover. Dwayne then decided to get some help to push it out. After his partner showed up, they walked to the aspen bluff where the buck had disappeared. Soon after, the buck broke from the cover, allowing Dwayne to get a crack at it. His shots missed, however, and the buck ran into posted land where Dwayne could not hunt.

The next day my son, Brad, and I cruised together in our truck. Walter and another fellow we hunt with, Walter Gamble, rode off in another vehicle. We saw several deer that day, and Brad made the group's first kill of the season, a 4x4 buck that he hit on the run from 200 yards. The bullet went through its lungs, dropping the buck a short distance later.

About 30 minutes before dusk, the two Walters saw the huge buck standing in posted land. The deer stood facing them on the crest of a hill about a half-mile from the road. They watched for a few minutes as the great buck stood silhouetted with two does nearby. He was at the edge of the posted land, and the fellows believed he was moving out of that field.

On the third day, Wednesday, Nov. 17, we were sure the buck had come out of the posted land, and so we searched hard for his tracks. After finding tracks we believed were his, we tracked him across a stubble field and into a nearby bluff. From there he moved into Rene's rye field. Unfortunately, we quickly lost his track because the field was full of deer tracks. Unlike many big bucks, this deer had small hooves, about the size of an average doe. This often made him difficult to track. We never saw the buck that day.

On the way to our place the next morning, Walter Meger spotted the buck again. He was driving slowly down a trail in his old 4x4 pickup when he saw deer ahead in a ditch and on the trail. He slowed down, stopped the truck, and looked at them. Suddenly he saw huge antlers emerging, but he could not see the buck's body because the deer was standing in a low spot on the trail. From what Walter could see, it looked like the buck everyone was talking about. He tried to get a better look, but the group spooked when he restarted his truck. Walter felt frustrated because the big buck had been standing on the trail he was driving on. The rolling terrain prevented him from seeing the whole animal.

Moments later, three does and a small 3-point buck ran

across the road about 100 yards in front of him. Running with them was the huge buck. All of the deer ran through a low area and into an aspen bluff. Walter never had a chance for a shot. If he had been coming from the other direction he likely would have seen the buck and possibly gotten a shot. Luck definitely plays a big part in hunting some days.

Walter and I hunted Friday and Saturday, Nov. 19 and 20, but we couldn't locate the big buck. However, we did see two bucks on Friday that we could have shot. They weren't spooky, and they stood about 100 yards inside a field looking at us. One was a decent 5-by-5 buck. It would have been an easy shot, but after considering both bucks, we decided to wait for a bigger deer, preferably the huge guy we knew was around.

Chapter 7

The Fateful Hunting Season: Week 2

Saskatchewan doesn't allow hunting on Sundays, and so our next available day was Monday, Nov. 22. As the week began, we still didn't have fresh snow. I decided to take care of some business in town and catch up on some chores that could no longer be ignored. Walter hunted that day with Rene and John, who had just returned from a moose hunt up north. None of the fellows saw anything they wanted to shoot.

Finally, the weather started to change late in the day. Heavy clouds came in from the west, carrying with them the promise of fresh snow. John called that evening to arrange a hunt, and said he would come over to pick me up the next morning. That night we got the snow we had been hoping for. It was just enough to cover all the old deer tracks. Conditions were ideal.

Walter Meger came to our house early that day, which was Tuesday, Nov. 23. As he came down the lane to the farm he saw a small, rut-crazed 4-by-4 buck with three does at a barley pile I had left about 200 yards from our house. Walter and I talked while drinking our morning coffee, and I told him I would hunt with John after I finished feeding the cattle. Walter drove over to pick up Rene, arriving just in time to catch the good early morning hunting light.

They had just left Rene's farm when they saw the big buck standing in a stubble field with two does. The deer were on the field's far side, several hundred yards away. Walter and Rene slipped out of the truck and got set up for a shot. Both of them ended up shooting several rounds, but they didn't hit the big buck. The shooting caused the does to run into nearby cover, but the buck split off and ran into a different poplar patch, which didn't surprise Walter and Rene. We've noticed that big bucks frequently sneak away from other deer when pressured.

Walter and Rene got back into the truck and drove around so they could look at the cover where the buck had run. They could not see him, but they also couldn't find any sign that he had run on through.

A few minutes after they finished looking for sign, John and I drove up. They excitedly told us their story, describing everything that had just happened. We quickly decided to do some pushes, so Rene took the buck's track and the rest of us traveled to sites that would allow us a good view and clear shooting. Rene had just entered the first bluff when the buck ran out. This was the first time I had ever seen him. His rack was extraordinary — which was obvious even at a great distance! Walter, John and I all took shots as the buck ran off, but no one connected.

Minutes later Rene emerged from the brush and said he had never seen the buck, but easily figured out what had happened when he heard the shooting. John reported that he had seen a deer moving in the heavy brush, but he couldn't see antlers and didn't try a shot until the buck broke out.

After we missed him, the buck ran across a field and into a pasture. The pasture covered about 100 acres, and contained several aspen bluffs. We found a set of tracks crossing a road nearby, but they didn't look fresh or large, so we weren't sure if they belonged to the buck or not. Because we weren't sure these were the buck's tracks, Rene and I returned to where we last saw him and followed his tracks to the road. We now had no doubt: These average- to under-sized tracks belonged to the buck.

We continued tracking him.

He crossed the road into a rye field but then mixed in with the tracks of several other deer. We soon lost him! Too many fresh tracks now crisscrossed the field. Because there was virtually no cover, we figured he must have gone into the adjacent hayfield, which was dotted with lots of brush and aspen bluffs.

The buck remained lost to us for a while. We were disappointed, but figured our best bet was to methodically start pushing nearby bluffs in hopes of flushing him back into the open. Not long after, Walter saw the buck suddenly run across the field. The buck crossed the rye field again, jumped a fence, and crossed one of my stubble fields. From there he ran into a big willow slough.

We followed him into the slough. We now knew where he was going. He was in an area all of us had hunted for many years. We knew every bluff and willow run, and we had a good idea where deer liked to move in this area. We quickly drove around to look for his tracks, and found them again. Once more, Rene began following the tracks while Walter drove around to the east side. Meanwhile, John and I drove to the northwest to make sure the buck didn't come out. The three of us then took up positions again, and waited for Rene to push through.

A short while later, John and I saw the buck pop out. We both fired several times but missed the hard-running buck

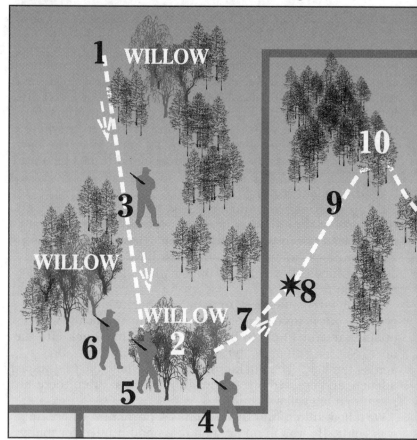

The fateful hunt for the world-record buck began shortly after dawn on Nov. 23, 1993, when Milo Hanson's hunting partners, Walter Meger and Rene Igini, spotted the buck with two does (1). After they shot several times at the buck, it ran to a stand of willows (2). Shortly after, Milo and John Yaroshko arrived in their truck. Walter stood guard west of the willows (3), while John Yaroshko covered the east escape (4) and Milo the south escape (5). Rene followed the buck's tracks into the willows (6).

Shortly after, the buck burst from the willows and ran northwest (7). Walter, John and Milo shot at the buck (8) as it headed across a large field of rye (9), but none of their shots connected. After the buck reached a far pasture that was covered with scattered aspen bluffs, the group lost the buck's average-sized tracks among other deer tracks (10). As the group began checking each aspen bluff, Walter saw the buck run across a field (11), cross onto Milo's property (12)

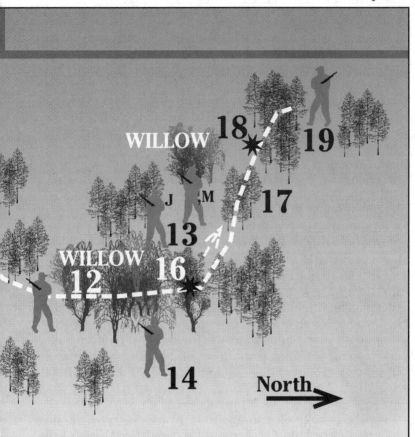

and enter a willow run.

John and Milo took up positions west of the willows (13), while Walter positioned himself to the east (14). Rene then followed the buck's tracks into the willows (15). The buck dashed from the brush and raced past Milo and John at about 150 yards, giving both of them broadside shots, which missed (16). The buck ran to the north and moved into a set of three aspen bluffs. Milo moved up to the third bluff and Rene walked through the southwest bluff (17).

When the buck ran out, it raced straight away from Milo. One of Milo's bullets knocked the buck to its knees (18), but it quickly got back up and ran about 450 yards to another aspen bluff (19). Milo and John followed, and Milo administered a neck shot after spotting the buck 50 yards away in the brush. A follow-up shot put the buck down for good.

as he raced across the field broadside at about 150 yards. The buck quickly covered the gap between the cover he had just escaped and another aspen bluff about 150 yards away.

This bluff was extremely thick. We briefly discussed our next push, and then circled the bluff and took up new positions. Rene again stayed on the track, while Walter moved to the east side, and John and I went to the northwest side. I trotted up to the bluff's point, and then waited for Rene to push through.

My heart was pumping, and the adrenaline was flowing, both from the run and the excitement of being so close to an incredible buck. Suddenly the buck bolted from the brush, raced into the field, and turned straight away from me at about 100 yards. I was amazed how fast he moved across the space before me!

At my first shot I saw a whitish, steamy cloud burst briefly into the air above his right side. I'm still not sure if this was an explosion of cut hair or antler material. Or had the bullet cut through some muscle, causing heat to escape, which produced a wisp of steam in the frigid air? Whatever happened, the great buck went down on his knees for a second, but quickly regained his feet and ran off. John saw the hit and yelled, "You got him!" Still, the buck was running on all four legs and looked as strong as ever.

I watched the buck run about 450 yards before disappearing into another bluff. John and I moved ahead toward the bluff as Walter walked out to get his truck. He and Rene then drove to the west side of the bluff. When John and I reached the bluff we were on a high point. I immediately saw the buck standing up and facing toward me only 50 yards away! I aimed for his neck and fired a shot that angled down into his chest. The great buck disappeared instantly, so I ran down to where he had been standing. I saw him on the far side of some blow-downs, about 15 to 20 feet from where I had last seen him. His head was still up, so I shot again to finish him off. My final bullet hit just behind the first verte-

Although Milo was jubilant after bagging the Hanson Buck, shown here, no one in his hunting party dreamed this deer was destined to become a new world record.

bra near the bottom of his skull. Now shaking, I walked over to him and was overwhelmed by the size of his rack. After looking at this huge buck for a minute, I heard Walter shout, "Did you get him?"

"You bet I did!" I shouted back.

I was soon joined by the other fellows. We all stood there admiring the huge antlers. Walter said: "Your bullet hit his antler. Look at the crack!"

I looked at the crack and the impact area and said, "Let's be careful when we drag him out, especially at the fence!"

We grabbed his antlers and started hauling. I was surprised how easily he pulled. I was so excited I could have dragged out a bull moose by myself! When we reached the truck, my hands were shaking badly. I asked John for a cigarette. I needed something to calm my nerves, even though I hadn't smoked for more than three years!

We then talked about the buck for a few minutes, and recounted the hunt one more time. Needless to say, everyone was excited about the buck's size. We agreed he was the biggest any of us had ever seen. Still, none of us ever dreamed this buck was destined to be a world record. After we were talked out, the boys helped me field-dress the buck. I tagged it, and we loaded the carcass into my truck.

We drove to my home, unloaded the buck in the yard, and then took some pictures with Olive's camera. While we were photographing, Brad drove up and took several photos with his camera.

We didn't know it then, but we were lucky Brad had shown up with his camera. Olive's camera had been empty, and I didn't know how to check to see if it contained film! Most of Brad's pictures turned out, though, and so we have some photos to help us remember that exciting day. We hung the buck from the crane I use in my shop, and then made a big lunch. A short while later we resumed hunting, this time taking Olive along. Even as we headed out, however, we had lost our enthusiasm for the hunt. We knew we had killed the biggest buck the area had to offer. I remember saying it was too bad we couldn't have "catch and release" for big bucks. That way we would have something to anticipate.

As we headed back out that afternoon, we ran into Gerald Malazdrewich. We told him we had shot the big buck everyone had been talking about, and that he might as well go home! Gerald drove to my shop and looked at the buck. He was so impressed that he brought out several guys during the next few days to see the magnificent rack.

44

Chapter 8

Reflections on the Hanson Buck

After I shot the Hanson Buck, I heard several opinions about its origin. Personally, even though I never saw the buck until the day I shot him, I believe he was born in our immediate area. Still others believe he was born far away and wandered into our area, possibly as a yearling buck. No one will ever know for sure. But from what we can tell, he lived most of his adult life in a 4- or 5-square-mile area around our farms. No doubt we haven't heard from everyone who saw the buck alive, but sometimes it seems that every-one who saw him alive enjoys telling people about the buck's oversized antlers.

During Summer 1993 almost everyone in our area heard about the huge buck. Because his antlers grew so large by that summer, it's obvious people paid attention when they sighted him. Another thing that made him noticeable was

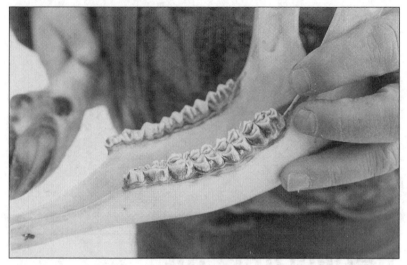

Surprised? Biologists who examined the Hanson Buck's jaw agree that the animal was probably only 4.5 years old.

that he seemed to feed in barley and field-pea fields in decent light. People spotted him feeding well into the morning and later in the afternoon. Obviously, the buck didn't seem to avoid feeding in open areas, and sometimes he was spotted close to roads or trails. He was also spotted occasionally near the blacktop highway north of Biggar. I am not aware of anyone ever seeing him after dark.

People in the coffee shop talked continually about this huge buck, and I don't doubt the coffee-talk increased the number of people who planned to seriously hunt him. Although he was well-known, I would not say he had become a legend by 1993 — as some local bucks had become in the past. After all, the locals hadn't named him, as they had a buck they dubbed the "Argo Buck." This buck was spotted southwest of town for many years. In fact, the buck lived so long that some of us suspect a succession of bucks were actually responsible for the Argo Buck's legend.

After I killed the Hanson Buck, I wanted to learn as much as possible about this great whitetail. My interest in the buck's background increased even further when I realized the buck was a potential Boone & Crockett world record. Ian McMurchy, who works for the Saskatchewan Environment and Resource Management, contacted me. He arranged for a biologist to accurately determine the buck's age. The man he contacted was Wally Kost, our regional wildlife biologist. When Wally examined the lower jaw, he was confident the buck was only about 4.5 years old, something that surprised me and many other people.

When Ian first called Wally to ask if he was interested in aging the buck, Wally asked if we would bring the antlers to Saskatoon with the jaw. That's when Ian explained it wouldn't be that easy. To ensure nothing happened to the buck's head, I was not letting it out of the vault in Biggar. When Wally heard that, he was on his way out the door! He knew then that this was not just another big buck.

"I wanted to be able to tell my kids I had held the world record white-tailed deer!" Wally said.

Wally was nervous as he drove west toward Biggar. He had aged a lot of deer over the years, but molar wear is not an exact science, no matter what you hear. That is especially true in the older age classes, which require subjective interpretation. Wally, like most people who heard about the buck, assumed the new world record must be an old deer. He was in store for a big surprise.

"When Milo brought out the jaw, I thought he was kidding," Wally said. "This was the jaw of a young deer with very little molar wear. But Milo assured me this was the Hanson Buck's jaw. The molar wear indicated it was only 4-and-one-half years old."

Wally, Ian and I talked about the factors that contributed to the young buck's massive antler development. Several environmental factors probably helped, especially the recent mild winters and an increase in legume crops produced in

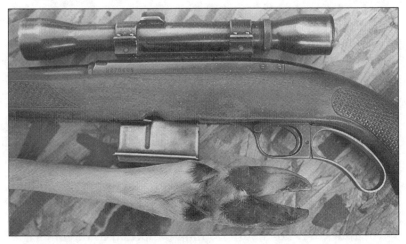

The Hanson Buck had relatively small hooves, and pads that were almost white.

the area.

Like most who have seen the antlers in person, Wally vividly recalls the special moment he first saw it.

"As Milo backed out of the vault, the rear tines appeared first, and I thought it was a mule deer," he said. "The antlers were much wider than the vault's door, and Milo had to hold them sideways to get out! Only when I held the rack and it framed my head and shoulders could I fully appreciate its sheer size. And all the time, Milo watched like a nervous parent. Awesome!"

Wally was the first biologist to age the jaw, but others followed. In January 1994, Olive and I flew to Dallas to attend the Shooting, Hunting and Outdoor Trade Show. I brought the jaw along, and showed it to some deer experts. Although some said it could pass for a 3.5-year-old buck, the consensus was that he was about 4.5 years old when he died.

The Hanson Buck had some other special characteristics that continue to fascinate me. When I first laid eyes on the buck, I was struck by the fact he did not have a large body, especially when compared to many big bucks I've seen in our area. No doubt his antlers are enormous and dominated his appearance, but he was not a huge, husky buck. I often rerun the memories of that special day, and still recall the enormous antlers and the body that didn't match the oversize headgear.

Another interesting aspect of the Hanson Buck is its average-size hooves. We first noticed this discrepancy when tracking him that day. Later, after I shot him, we looked at his hooves closely and agreed they were about

A bullet fragment caused a 1.5-inch crack in the Hanson Buck's right antler beam. The fragment remains lodged in the antler.

the size of an average white-tailed doe in our area. Also, the pads that form the bottom of each hoof were unique because they were almost white instead of the normal black. I've never seen such light-colored pads on any deer in this area. I have seen many bucks, alive and mounted, and have always believed the Hanson Buck had the looks of a young, fine-featured animal. Also, his rack is extremely wide and high, so much so that many people believe the rack is a bit light in the main beams. This really isn't so. In fact, his main beams approach 5 inches in circumference. His rack just looks thin because of its great height and width. The antlers are also light in color, not darkly stained like white-tailed bucks from farther north in the forest.

I will always remain a bit concerned about the integrity of

the rack's right main beam. That's because of the bullet hole
and a fragment from the bullet itself. The bullet caused a
1.5-inch crack near the impact site, so we always handle the
rack carefully. The crack's exact location is between the G1
and G2 tines, almost centered on the back of the main beam.
At the crack's base is a neat round hole with the bullet fragment embedded just below the surface. The impact blew
away antler material from a 2- to 3-inch area around the
bullet hole. Another bullet fragment blew more antler material away from the base of the G2 tine, and there is a tiny
impact site about half way up the G2.

Though concerned about the crack, I have never really worried the main beam would actually break. After all, we
dragged the buck by both antlers when we first moved him.
Still, now that I know he is the world's record whitetail, I
handle his rack much more carefully. No one needs to tell
me how lucky I am that the rack wasn't broken by the bullet
or subsequent handling. As a precaution, I now keep the
entire impact site heavily taped for additional strength. I use
camo tape for this "brace," and some people don't even notice
the tape when we display the head.

Most sportsmen know the story but they still ask about the
tape. Now that the buck has been panel-scored by the Boone
& Crockett Club, my taxidermist, Bub Hill, and I will look at
reinforcing the main beam so it will never break. The rein-
forcement will be discreet because I do not want to alter the
outward appearance of the bullet's impact area. After all, the
bullet damage is a part of the Hanson Buck's history.

A final comment about this famous buck: Many people
have asked how the venison tasted. The meat was not tough
or "gamey" tasting. Also, much of the meat was made into
sausage, and it's as good as any we've eaten.

Chapter 9

A Record Realized

After the Hanson Buck fell on Nov. 23, 1993, the next four days turned out to be the last normal moments Olive and I would enjoy for quite some time. The following day, I drove to the nearby town of Perdue to buy a non-trophy tag for white-tails. This license would allow me to keep hunting for antler-less deer.

I then resumed hunting with Walter Meger and various neighbors. I was mostly interested in helping my buddies find some bucks. We hunted hard but didn't shoot anything.

Meanwhile, many folks wanted to hear about my big buck, and I was often asked how high his rack scored. I told every-one I thought it would score in the 190s, which would be incredible by anyone's standards. In the days that followed, I became increasingly curious about his actual score, but I never thought once that he would somehow be a new world

51

record. Had we known that's what we had hanging in my shop, Olive and I would have made sure we enjoyed those four post-hunt days. It never occurred to us that our life was about to change dramatically.

During those four days, the Hanson Buck hung from the overhead crane in my shop. And for much of the time that Olive and I were out hunting, we left the shop open. We never considered that someone might want to steal the big buck. Several neighbors and friends came over to look at his rack. Of course, no one even mentioned the crazy idea that this could be a world record. Something like that just doesn't happen to someone you know, let alone yourself!

On Nov. 27, Walter and I removed the head and cape, and left the carcass hanging from the crane. The head and rack spent that evening on the shop's floor.

On Nov. 28 about 3 p.m., our good friend Adam Evashenko came over to score my buck. Adam had scored big game for the Biggar Wildlife Federation for 15 years, and I knew he would be accurate. He is a self-taught scorer, and over the years he has measured many deer, moose and elk. I helped hold and position the buck's head on my truck's tailgate while Adam measured the rack. Walter, meanwhile, wrote down the measurements as Adam told him the scores. The job went quickly because the buck's uniform, typical rack is "clean," with few tricky measurements. No doubt the weather also played a role in Adam's fast work, because we were standing outside in minus 30-degree temperatures!

After the measurements were made and recorded, we went inside to add up the score. Adam seemed puzzled when he finished the task. He said he might have screwed up adding the fractions, and so he asked me to recheck his adding. Olive and I went through each number and came up with the same total. We rechecked the adding again, and still got the same number: 214 even!

Adam looked at me and said: "I think you have the new world record. You have it beat by a long way." After all, the famous Jordan Buck, killed in 1914 in Wisconsin, scores 206-1/8. The Jordan Buck had held the No. 1 spot since being entered in the Boone & Crockett record book in 1971.

Adam remembers that I laughed, then my face went blank, and then I let out a bigger laugh. I was so excited I needed to celebrate, so we opened a bottle of rum and savored the moment.

I knew before that moment that I needed to have the antlers scored for the Biggar Wildlife Federation trophy night. I wanted Bruce Kushner, the current club scorer, to measure the rack for my entry. Adam asked me not to tell Bruce the rack had already been scored. That would allow us to compare the two scores without Bruce being influenced by Adam's number.

I called Bruce the next day, and he invited me to bring the rack to his home after supper. Olive and I took the head over to his farm, which is about six miles northwest of our place. We went into his garage, where Bruce quickly measured and recorded the numbers. When he finished, we went into his home and he added up his measurements. He mentioned he had heard the buck scored in the 190s, and he expected the final tally would be in that range.

Moments later, his face went white and he said, "I must have made a mistake because my score is over 215." I told him Adam had scored it at 214 even. Bruce rechecked all the numbers and columns and came up with 214-6/8. He became very excited, and then called his father and some relatives to come see the rack. His dad studied the antlers for a while and then offered me $50,000! I don't know how serious he was, but this was the first offer the Hanson Buck attracted.

After Olive and I arrived home, I hid the head and antlers deep inside a large pile of barley grain near the yard. Looking back, I realize I became a little paranoid about the head's security. Olive and I went through some anxious moments as we tried to understand and appreciate what was involved in having a potential world-record whitetail in our possession. We couldn't comprehend how valuable it was, and how protective we had to become. During the next few days, we hid the rack in combine hoppers, grain piles and other strange places around the farm. The antlers became a headache for us. We needed to get them into secure storage.

While we were at Bruce's home, he had called another scorer, Jim Wiebe. Bruce suggested Jim visit us and do a third independent measurement. On the evening of Nov. 30, Jim and Bruce came over to score the antlers.

Jim is the scorer for a big-buck contest at the nearby hamlet of Sonningdale. After he scored the rack, he asked me to bring it to their annual big-buck night on Dec. 3.

Jim scored the antlers at 215-5/8, dispelling his skepticism over the buck's record-class score. Why was his score slightly higher than those recorded by Adam and Bruce? Unlike them, Jim didn't count one of the stickers as a tine. Under the Boone & Crockett Club's sometimes complicated scoring system, tines that aren't "matched" on the other antler are counted as deductions. Jim's interpretation of the sticker points made his score slightly higher than the others.

I asked Jim to offer his recollections of scoring the Hanson Buck that night. His comments follow:

"When Bruce (Kushner) called me, he sounded somewhat puzzled when he described scoring the rack. Bruce was confident in his scoring ability, yet he was having difficulty accepting that he had come up with numbers that exceeded the current world record.

"When I saw the antlers after arriving at the Hanson farm, I immediately was impressed with their clean and typical qualities. I was now sure that Bruce's measurements were accurate. Although antler scoring by Boone & Crockett procedure is fairly explicit, there will always be some judgment calls. In this case, though, I found the antlers to be easy to measure, except for the sticker on the brow tine.

"By Boone & Crockett definition, a tine must measure at

least 1 inch to be considered a tine, and it must be longer
than the width of its base. I believed the brow tine's sticker
did not exactly meet the B&C requirements, so I didn't
include it in my measurements. This tine can influence the
score by 1-1/8 inch. I am sure the scorers who include this
tine are using their best judgment, and perhaps they're being
as strict as possible. Either way, the Hanson Buck easily
qualifies as the world record."

As Jim scored the rack the night of Nov. 30, our garage
somehow became filled with deer hunters. We sat around
talking hunting for several hours. The fellows from the
wildlife club had driven out to the farm, and several of my
neighbors had come over to hear the results of another scoring. Everyone was in a good mood. The antlers were on a
table in the middle of the garage, and I remember someone
asking if we should bow to them.

I really didn't know anything about the Boone & Crockett
Club's procedures, so I asked a couple of fellows from the
Biggar Wildlife Federation if they could help me arrange an
official measurement. Murray Newton, the club's president,
contacted the closest official scorer he could find. That man
was Norm Parchewsky, who lived in Saskatoon at the time.

When Murray told Norm two people had rough-scored a
buck near Biggar at around 214, his first question was,
"Mule deer or non-typical whitetail?"

Murray told him: "No! It's a typical whitetail."

Norm then called me to get more information. Next he
called Joe Schmidt, a friend and fellow hunter, and invited
him to ride to Biggar on Dec. 1 to see the rack.

"Joe and I shared hunting stories during the ride, but the
conversation kept going back to the trophy we were going to
see," Norm said. 'What if it's not that big? Is it really a typical? Is the rack clean or controversial?' These were the questions we pondered. Every year we hear stories of a new world
record whitetail, but something invariably happens."

When Norm arrived at our farm that morning, my driveway

It takes two fellows to hold that rack. Bruce Kushner, left, and Norm Parchewsky pose Dec. 1, 1993, before Norm scored the Hanson Buck.

and yard were full of vehicles. He said he almost expected to see a parking lot attendant.

When he saw the buck's clean, massive rack, he knew why everyone had come. This rack definitely had the potential to be a world record. With the help of Jim and Bruce, he measured the Hanson Buck. Norm's green score that day ended up at 214-4/8. Norm spent the better part of the afternoon at my farm, and got to meet everyone from our hunting group.

"You couldn't help but realize how honest and down to earth these people were," Norm said later. "No one could be more deserving of this good fortune. The hunt itself was a good story, including the teamwork and events leading up to the final shot. They could all be proud. This buck was not

Seeing Norm Parchewsky between the Hanson Buck's massive antlers gives you a better appreciation for the rack's immense size.

shot with any controversy, nor was there anything negative to report about the people involved. They gave hunting and hunters a good name. This was a group of friends out enjoying the sport and sharing a common interest. The buck was their bonus."

When Norm returned home that night, he had several phone calls and messages. The Hanson Buck wasn't even his deer, yet outdoor writers, photographers and taxidermists phoned him during the next several days to pump him for information. This gave him a small taste of what Olive and I were going through.

Norm's score of 214-4/8 was entered that day with the Saskatchewan Henry Kelsey Club as the new Saskatchewan record. Unlike the Boone & Crockett Club, the Henry Kelsey Club has no mandatory 60-day drying period. Also, the Henry Kelsey score sheet differs slightly from the final B&C score sheet.

Chapter 10

Shoot a World Record and They Will Come

After lunch on Dec. 1, a TV camera crew arrived and Norm re-enacted the scoring he had performed that morning. Then the interviewer talked to him and Jim Wiebe. When my turn came, I was extremely nervous. This was the first TV interview of my life! After I talked with the TV people, I went into the house and Olive asked me what I said. I told her I didn't have a clue. We would have to watch it on TV!

All of my hunting buddies and several executives from the wildlife club had come over to watch. My partners had been hunting all morning and, after the measuring, they went back to hunting. I spent the day visiting with many other fellows who came by to see the antlers and offer me congratulations. Olive and I were extremely nervous because we just weren't used to having so many people, both friends and total strangers, in our home. That day was the beginning of

59

You might say the new world-record whitetail generated some interest. The Hansons received numerous calls and letters along with inquiries from the hunting media. Several magazine articles followed.

one of the most trying periods of our lives.

After Jim had measured the antlers the night before, he asked if I minded if he called a magazine about the big buck. I didn't object, so he made the call. Before I knew it, I was getting calls from several magazines and outdoor writers. Then, to our amazement, two men from *North American Whitetail* magazine arrived from Georgia with Jim. They were excited about the head, and wanted me to sign an agreement for exclusive magazine rights to my story.

I became quite stressed that day because, while they were in the house, one of the largest outdoor magazines in the United States was calling and trying to negotiate a similar deal! The Southerners were persistent fellows, though, and late that evening we made a deal.

Another reason for my anxiety was yet another unexpected visit that day: Right in the middle of all the magazine business, an officer from the Royal Canadian Mounted Police arrived. He congratulated me, and said he was just stopping by to ensure I realized the importance of safe-keeping. He mentioned that I should consider secure storage. He said that because the rack had such a high potential value, and thousands of people were quickly hearing about it, the farm

Although he had never done a television interview before he shot the Hanson Buck, Milo soon found himself growing accustomed to life in front of numerous cameras. Here, he and Bill Jordan relax in between filming sessions for the Realtree Outdoors TV show.

might not be the best place to keep it. He said the RCMP was aware that high-scoring deer racks occasionally get stolen. Although his visit was polite and merely precautionary, I really started to get uptight about the antlers' security. I later hid the antlers carefully, but didn't sleep well at all that night.

The next day, Dec. 2, the phone started ringing about 6 a.m. We had to do something to get a break from the calls. Our neighbor Wayne Yaroshko brought over an answering machine and hooked it up to the kitchen phone so we wouldn't have to answer every call. We could now at least have a coffee or a meal without continually talking on the phone. The machine also allowed us to monitor the calls so we could

After bagging the Hanson Buck, Milo spent quite a bit of time on the telephone with writers, editors and other white-tail deer enthusiasts.

talk to friends and neighbors. That is, if they could get through.

That afternoon, a field editor from *Outdoor Life* magazine arrived at our home. He had been hunting in Saskatchewan and was on his way home to Wyoming. We began working on a second-rights agreement for my story. Jim came over that evening and caped out the head so we could get the hide frozen. I remained concerned about security for the antlers, and realized I couldn't continue moving the head around between hiding places on the farm. I talked with Murray Newton and Dave Pickett from the Wildlife Federation, and they started looking for a vault or some other secure storage.

Dec. 3 was yet another big day for us. Our friend Mike Kostuchenko had built a large plywood box that would hold the antlers for transportation and viewing as we prepared to

Although the media kept Milo busy with interviews and photo requests, he still had chores to tend to on his farm. Here, he uses a four-wheel-drive tractor to load hay bales for his cattle.

take the rack to its first public display at Sonningdale that night. My hunting buddies arrived around 5 p.m., and we immediately found the display box was slightly too large to fit into John Yaroshko's Suburban truck. That meant we had to haul it in the back of a pickup truck, which concerned me. I was afraid it might blow out and be destroyed. I don't think I was being paranoid. A nasty blizzard had blown in, and the trip would be difficult. We had to drive slowly because visibility was poor.

After we arrived at the show, I really enjoyed myself. That was the first time I had relaxed for a few days. I won the trophy that night for the area's largest typical rack, and I also received a high-quality hunting knife. We met a lot of nice people and returned home after midnight. Several of the guys ended up at our place, and we talked hunting until the wee hours.

Dec. 4 and Dec. 5 were reasonably quiet, except the phone still rang continuously. Until then we didn't know that a telephone could become such a focus in a person's life. Virtually

News of the Hanson Buck spread like wildfire. Local and national media chronicled nearly every breaking event in the buck's story.

every minute of the day, the phone was either ringing or the answering machine was recording a message. Whenever possible, I tried to answer or return the calls, but I never caught up. There were so many calls that I would not have had time to do anything except talk on the phone.

For the first time in our lives, Olive and I had so many things going on that we had to buy a day planner to keep track of appointments. Meanwhile, I tried to catch up on chores because, through all this, I still had 100 cows to feed, regardless of the time or how busy I was with other things. Some days I couldn't get at the feeding until after midnight. The cows didn't seem to mind, though. To feed them, I use the tractor to haul big round alfalfa bales into the corral. Each bale weighs about 1,200 pounds, and the cattle consume four bales daily.

On Dec. 6, I received a call from the Saskatchewan

Environment and Resource Management department. Ian McMurchy from the wildlife branch in Regina called to suggest a meeting, and we agreed that he would drive up to the farm in a couple of days.

That afternoon, Olive and I met with Murray and Dave, and we looked for a vault in Biggar. I brought the buck's head with me, and a local part-time taxidermist, Al Ashkar, thoroughly cleaned and salted the skull to ensure nothing would rot. Al didn't boil the skull to clean it because we were concerned about shrinkage and changing some measurements. Dave kept the head at his house that night, and I enjoyed my best sleep in about a week. Unfortunately for Dave, he didn't sleep a wink. He found it nerve racking to have a potential world-record white-tailed deer rack in his possession. Now he knew how I had been feeling!

The next day, Dec. 7, was like all of the previous week, with constant phone calls and interruptions. I imagine that the telephone company's information operators got tired of handling requests for our telephone number. I met Dave after lunch, and we placed the buck's head in a vault at an old rural municipality building that the school division used for storage.

We had a waiver drafted just in case the place burned down, or something equally disastrous happened. The school division did not want to be liable for the rack's security, and I understood completely. When we got home we felt relieved that the antlers were safely stored, but we were getting exhausted by everything.

On Dec. 9, we received a fax of the first draft of the *North American Whitetail* article on the Hanson Buck. This still seems amazing. Only 17 days had passed since the buck was killed, and here we were proofing a magazine article that described the hunt. We also received confirmation that the magazine was preparing a second article, so I stayed busy with the editors and writers.

During these days, I repeatedly had to deny information to

many people because of my contract obligations to these first two magazines. Olive and I drove into Saskatoon at one point to talk with our lawyer about all of the events taking place. After our meeting, we returned home for our first visit with Ian McMurchy. Among other things, Ian explained the legalities of transporting or selling the rack, and he told us the provincial government wanted to obtain a promotional photo when the buck was mounted. Because Ian is also a frequently published free-lance wildlife photographer, he has extensive knowledge of the magazine industry, not to mention the white-tailed deer "industry." Olive and I took many notes during these conversations. We had a lot of questions that required knowledgeable answers. Therefore, we were relieved to talk with someone who could explain our rights and give us a better understanding of the world we were now in — whether we wanted to be in that world or not!

After Ian left, we still had chores to do, which included proof-reading the first magazine manuscript. We didn't get to bed until 3 a.m. We were exhausted.

We got away from the farm and the big-deer pressures for a few days when we went down to Shaunavon for my father's birthday. But even there we constantly talked about the big buck. When we returned home, the calls had slowed down a bit. We tried to get back into our old routine. Still, we continued to receive offers, and needed to make decisions. We were even invited to attend the huge Shooting, Hunting and Outdoor Trade Show in Dallas, Texas, as guests of *North American Whitetail*. I also attended local meetings with several organizations to develop ideas that would enable the area and town to benefit from the Hanson Buck.

I continued to talk to Ian and seek his counsel about the many things that were happening. I'll always remember the morning he brought Wally Kost, the Saskatoon regional biologist, to see the skull and antlers. They were impressed when they saw the rack, but neither fellow dared to touch it. At the time, I had a heavy wrap of electrical tape on the beam hit by the bullet, so they didn't know how fragile the rack really was.

Ian and I had a long, detailed talk about the taxidermy job the buck would require. On his recommendation, I decided to talk with Bub Hill from Briercrest, Saskatchewan. I thought that perhaps Bub and Al could do the job, so Al and I drove down to meet Bub. He agreed to do the work, and I left the cape with him on Dec. 20.

After returning home, we had a nice family Christmas. The boys were home, and lots of friends kept stopping by. Needless to say, the buck was discussed frequently. Life was normal for a while, except for our preparations for the trip to Dallas. I caught up on lots of work that had been set aside, and we made sure the boys knew what was required while we were gone.

I even had time to meet Ian and Bub in Saskatoon one afternoon. We discussed two essential tasks: the taxidermy job and the photography to document the Hanson Buck. The fellows were well-prepared, and our meeting went smoothly. Bub had a sketch of the optimum mount, and he explained how to best display the buck. Ian listed all of the photo requirements we had discussed, and outlined how he would carry out the shoots. I was confident both men were capable of doing the high-quality work the buck required. They were good people to work with, and helped me take care of two big headaches in one meeting.

Around Jan. 10, 1994, the first magazine article on the Hanson Buck hit the newsstands. The days of non-stop phone calls resumed. We left for Dallas the next day, however, so we weren't aware of the calls at first. We soon found out that our answering machine was filling up daily.

We left Saskatoon in minus 30-degree weather on Jan. 11, and arrived in 70-degree warmth in Dallas. The warm weather and beautiful surroundings made us forget Saskatchewan for a few days. We met many nice people at the SHOT Show, and were impressed and amazed by the importance of white-tailed deer trophies to some folks. I spent so much time autographing magazine covers that I didn't have time to see the show.

Before we knew it, we were back on the jet and flying home. As soon as we returned we met with the local Wildlife Federation fellows to begin planning the official scoring ceremony. About the same time, Ian talked to some friends of his at Realtree Outdoors. Bill Jordan and I agreed to do a video segment and TV show on the Hanson Buck, starting with the scoring ceremony.

I feel fortunate to live near a town with such an active wildlife club. I have been a member of this federation for many years. As one of its 500-plus members, I firmly believe the club has always taken on worthwhile projects. They accomplish a great deal for our area's fish and wildlife. The club is particularly interested in preserving local wildlife habitat, and ensuring that the great diversity of wildlife is maintained for future generations. The federation helped obtain a lot of Wildlife Development Fund Land in our area, and I'm sure this land helps ensure more white-tailed bucks reach maturity.

The federation's members also understood how important the Hanson Buck could be for the community, and they lead the way in every way possible to help generate support for area projects. I'm always pleased to cooperate in any way because I think it's important to support local conservation efforts. I'm glad the Hanson Buck can benefit our area, and I sincerely hope people regard this world-record deer as a good thing for Biggar and Saskatchewan.

Chapter 11

The 60-Day Official Scoring Ceremony

I'll never forget Jan. 22, 1994. That was the day the Boone & Crockett Club's 60-day drying period ended. As a result, it was also the day the Biggar Wildlife Federation scheduled the official Boone & Crockett scoring ceremony, which took place at the Biggar High School auditorium.

We expected many media people to cover the event, including radio reporters, national TV network crews, and newspaper and magazine writers. The group also included David Blanton, the cameraman for Realtree Outdoors TV, who came all the way from Georgia. In addition to the professional media, my neighbor Wayne Yaroshko would shoot a video production of the Hanson Buck's history, which included the scoring ceremony.

Ian McMurchy would also be on hand to photograph the scoring ceremony, not to mention the taxidermy work that

*More than 400 people — including numerous media represen-
tatives — attended the Hanson Buck's official Boone and
Crockett scoring ceremony on Jan. 22, 1994, in Biggar.*

would begin immediately that night when the ceremony
ended. And finally, Ian would photograph the buck's final
mounted portraits on prints and slides. We had thorough
coverage of the Hanson Buck!

The scoring ceremony became a wonderful reunion. Many
family members, and old and new friends showed up. In
addition, one of my oldest friends, Robert Allemand, accepted
my invitation to be part of the Boone & Crockett Club's
three-man scoring panel. He is a rancher from the Eastend,
Saskatchewan, area, and we grew up together. Another old
friend from those days, Wally Envik, agreed to be master of
ceremonies. He ranches near Shaunavon, and is a past president of the Saskatchewan Wildlife Federation. Wally was our
best man when Olive and I were married. Besides all that,
Wally and Robert are great sportsmen, and so I was proud to

have them share this day.

The ceremony also allowed me to contribute to a good fund-raising opportunity for the wildlife club, and to thank its members for all their work. I had brought back a large supply of the magazine that published the first story of the Hanson Buck. The evening before the ceremony, our hunting party had met at my farm to autograph 100 issues and put them into protective plastic bags. I autographed another 300 copies, and all these magazines were sold at the ceremony. The magazines autographed by our hunting group sold for $20 each! The club set aside the money for habitat projects.

I came to rely on Murray Newton and Dave Pickett during those hectic weeks after I shot the buck. The scoring ceremony was a perfect example of how these men make good things happen. The evening before the ceremony, several club members met at the high school. We set up tables and chairs on the stage and got everything ready for the big day.

The next morning I took the buck's head out of the vault and locked it inside a secure room in the high school. Everything started coming together as the camera crews, media, scorers, dignitaries, friends and family members showed up. I was amazed at the number of people who attended. Well more than 400 people filled the auditorium.

I sat behind a table at the entrance and autographed magazines for more than an hour before the ceremony. I think I greeted just about everyone who entered. I had signed a few autographs at the SHOT Show in Dallas, Texas, earlier that month, but now almost everyone wanted me to sign their copy of the magazine.

That was my true introduction to autograph signing, and it was something that required adjustment. It certainly didn't come naturally! I had never thought anyone would want my autograph — except maybe the bank.

Mounted deer heads adorned the auditorium's walls to help set the proper atmosphere for the event. When the scoring was about to begin, our special guests took their seats along

Milo doesn't remember what he said after his record buck was scored Jan. 22, 1993. He does remember being relieved and happy that the rack's score didn't change much from the initial measurements taken two months earlier.

one side and across the back of the large, elevated stage. The scoring took place on a table at the stage's center near the front. Everyone had a good view.

The wildlife club had prepared information posters to help the crowd understand what was taking place. The posters explained the scoring process, and they included a score sheet from the then-world record, the famous Jordan Buck. Federation members had also prepared a huge, blank score sheet for the Hanson buck, and mounted it high on a wall beside the stage. As the measurements were verified, club president Murray Newton wrote in the scores for all to see. Wayne and his partner, Rod Meger, had even set up a closed-circuit TV broadcast. Several TV monitors around the auditorium showed the scoring as it progressed.

Vern Klein, a longtime wildlife club member, introduced everyone on the stage, and described how much interest the Hanson Buck had generated. We then heard from Biggar's mayor and our local legislator. Next, the province's minister of Environment and Resource Management congratulated me. Finally, the three official scorers were introduced. I then removed the electrical tape from the buck's left beam, and the scorers began measuring the rack.

The three scorers — Bob Allemand, Allen Holtvogt and Norm Parchewsky — are excellent professionals. Allen is from Anaheim, Saskatchewan, about two hours east of Biggar. Norm had called Allen on Jan. 21 to see if he would be part of the Hanson Buck's scoring panel.

"All I said was, 'When do I have to be there?' Allen recalls. "Never in my wildest dreams did I think I would have that opportunity. Needless to say, I was single-minded the rest of that day. All I could think about was the Hanson Buck. I greatly anticipated seeing and measuring a potential world record. I saw every hour on the alarm clock that night!"

After arriving in Biggar on Jan. 22 and receiving the necessary introductions and instructions, Allen took a seat on stage. As he watched people filing in and TV crews setting up, he said he began to feel he might be in over his head. But his anxiety disappeared once the measuring began.

"I realized it was the same as any other scoring day, except that 400 more people were watching, video cameras were running, and photographers kept snapping pictures," Allen said. "And in the middle of it all sat a 213-1/8-inch typical whitetail. I have always gotten a thrill out of measuring big racks and hearing the stories behind them. And this was the big one!"

Allen said he continues to hear many questions about the Hanson Buck, and enjoys the wild rumors that have circulated in the big buck's wake.

That day was also special for Bob, who farms and ranches in southwestern Saskatchewan. Bob, who has scored big-game racks since 1964, enjoys measuring trophies and listening to all the hunting stories. In 1989, the Henry Kelsey Club honored him with a plaque in recognition of his many years of service. And in November 1990 he attended and passed a four-day Boone & Crockett measurers' course to become an official measurer. Still, he never thought he would get a chance to score the Hanson Buck.

"I never imagined I would be one of the official scorers of a world-record whitetail, especially one taken by an old friend!" Bob said.

Bob and I attended the same one-room country school together. We played together even before we were old enough for school. As we grew older, we enjoyed the normal teen-age activities such as parties, cars and girls. After reaching adulthood, our lives took us in different directions until the Hanson Buck reunited us.

Norm Parchewsky also loves scoring big racks, explaining that it helped develop his philosophy of being "second best."

"By 'second best' I mean that if I am not putting my tag on one of these giants, I can still share the enjoyment of someone more fortunate by scoring their rack for them," Norm said. "I have been fortunate to measure some impressive antlers, including a beautiful 229-5/8 non-typical whitetail.

"Still, a trophy is in the eye of the person pulling the trigger or drawing the bow. The size of the rack doesn't always determine the hunter's pride. A first buck, a big doe or the trophy of a lifetime are all equal, except for the antlers, which are the bonus."

Norm said he'll never forget the tension when it came time to officially score the Hanson Buck with Allen and Bob.

"Pressure!" he said. "There was lots of pressure because we knew our measurement would be scrutinized with a magnifying glass. We measured each point several times, and carefully added the scores twice."

The official measuring went smoothly. When the scorers reached the brow tine's sticker, they talked it over and agreed it should be included and its score deducted. Each scorer worked intensely, but they relaxed as the scoring progressed. They realized they were getting their moments of fame. After all, only three men could say they measured the Hanson Buck at its 60-day scoring session.

As each measurement was recorded, the number was marked on the big score sheet. Everyone in the crowd talked quietly among themselves and watched. I was too nervous to sit still. I walked around the stage and talked to my hunting buddies or anyone else I recognized. The scoring seemed to take a long time. Wally Envik did a great job keeping the crowd informed, describing what the scorers were doing. Everyone waited anxiously for the strict decisions and exact measurements to be completed. I was aware of the TV guys moving about, and Ian McMurchy's camera flash going off. Mostly, though, I tried not to get too excited. Olive and Brad were in the crowd, but I didn't have a chance to talk with them.

Finally, the measuring completed, the scorers carefully computed the final score, and then repeated their checks.

"Our score was error-free both times, with no shortcuts and no compromise," Norm said. "We signed the forms only after we checked and rechecked the score. Our name goes on along with our reputation."

Finally, Envik informed the crowd that the scoring was completed. The official Boone & Crockett entry score was 213-1/8, a full 7 inches larger than the Jordan Buck! The crowd cheered and clapped when the final score was announced. I was relieved and happy, and surprised the score hadn't changed much from the initial measurements taken two months earlier.

Wally then asked me to say a few words. I don't remember much of anything that I said. I introduced my hunting partners and thanked them for all their help. They said later that they were just as nervous as I was. Several people told me I didn't appear nervous when I gave my speech. I guess my excitement disguised it well.

After the final score was determined, Norm asked me to sign the score sheets. Wally then invited everyone to the nearby Elks' hall for a celebration. I placed the rack into the back of the display box, and we moved the box to the stage's center. I then asked the fellows to remove the barricades in front of the stage so everyone could take a good look at the Hanson Buck. I visited with many well-wishers and even managed to talk to Olive and Brad. They were as happy as I was. Everyone in the room filed past the buck. About 30 minutes later, most of the people had left.

After the room was empty, I wrapped the head inside a sheet. Bub Hill then took it out and placed it into his car's trunk. Ian, Bub, Al Ashkar and Wayne drove out to my farm so Bub could start the taxidermy work. Ian, David and Wayne photographed and filmed the entire process.

My family traveled a long way to be with me that day. My father, E.O. Hanson; my brother, Dave; and two sisters, Gail and Ione, and their families shared our joy. We all went out to celebrate with a meal after the ceremony, and then we returned to the Elks' hall and visited people until midnight. Olive and I ended this long, memorable day by driving home to see how the taxidermy work was going.

Chapter 12

Recording the Hanson Buck on Film

Like most whitetails shot in North America, the Hanson Buck's image was captured on film shortly after its death. Although our first attempts at photos failed because the first camera we grabbed had no film, the picture-taking seldom slowed in the weeks and months that followed.

I'm confident no deer shot in modern times has been photographed more thoroughly than the Hanson Buck. The buck has been documented on video, color slides and prints. In partnership with a video crew and a handful of professional and amateur photographers, we have maintained control over almost all original images of the buck. These photographers have done a great service for all those deer hunters who can only see the buck through TV, videotape, magazines and newspapers.

Who are these photographers? Wayne Yaroshko is a valued

Milo believes the Hanson Buck has been photographed more than any other whitetail shot in modern history. Here, Ian McMurchy, right, the official photographer of the Hanson Buck, works to set up a photo shoot.

friend and neighbor. He and his partner, Rod Meger, run a video production company, and have followed the Hanson Buck from the start. They've taped virtually every Hanson Buck event as it happened. Wayne and Rod plan to produce and market a video of the Hanson Buck.

Ian McMurchy works for the Saskatchewan wildlife agency, and is a part-time free-lance photographer. Ian has worked on big-game projects and wildlife research for almost 30 years with the agency, and his photography has appeared in most of the continent's premier outdoor magazines the past few years. He is our official photographer, and our partner in marketing photography of the Hanson Buck. Ian's photos truly show the beauty of this wonderful buck.

Allow me to tell you more about Wayne Yaroshko and Ian McMurchy. Chances are, if you've seen a photo or video of the Hanson Buck, these men are responsible for the images you saw.

Wayne Yaroshko farms near me and Olive, and has been our friend since we began farming. His strong interest in electronics led him to try his first video cameras. It seems that even in those early years more people saw Wayne with a camera on his shoulder than without one. In the early 1980s, after taping a local production in town, he met Rod Meger, who is just about as crazy as Wayne about video. Rod lives about eight miles away from me on the other side of the highway.

Wayne, Rod and Larry Antonenko soon formed a partnership and began working together on various projects. The Yaroshko Meger Video Association (YMVA) continued to grow as they were helped by Rod's wife, Florette. Since 1991, Florette has regularly run the camera for their mobile productions. When more help is needed, another neighbor and friend, Don Zbeeshko, operates the cameras. This group tapes a variety of events, and produces videos for local businesses.

Wayne grew up in the Biggar area, and has hunted whitetails near home with various neighbors for years. Like most locals, he had heard about a huge buck north of town. His brother Gerry was the one who broke the news to him that I had shot the big buck, and that it was impressive. After Wayne heard the buck was record-sized, and that an official from Saskatoon was coming to score the rack, his mother asked Olive and me if we wanted YMVA to videotape the scoring. We agreed it was a good idea. Because Wayne had a previous engagement that day, Rod taped the event along with CFQC television and amateur videographers. Olive and I worked out a gentleman's agreement with YMVA for security of the videotapes.

A few days later, Wayne helped me prepare to take the head to Sonningdale's Big Buck Night. He printed signs that said, "No Photos Please," along with a huge banner that said, "Hanson Buck." We asked that no photos be taken at this public showing in order to maintain our contract agreement with the magazines that bought first- and second-time publication rights.

Wayne couldn't attend that event so Larry taped the proceedings. A couple of weeks later, we entered the head in another local buck night sponsored by the Westwinds Motor Hotel. Wayne showed up to videotape the event.

Until that time, Wayne and Rod had been shooting video they thought I would want for my personal enjoyment. After we became aware of the buck's importance, we discussed creating a "Hanson Buck Chronicle" that would be marketed to the public. We agreed I would have exclusive rights if a commercial video production was viable, and that we would work out a more formal agreement at the appropriate time.

The next big event was the official scoring ceremony after the Boone and Crockett Club's 60-day drying period. Wayne and Rod decided the best way to record the event was a full-blown three-camera mobile production. They set up their equipment the night before the ceremony, and their mobile "shack" controlled the footage shown on the auditorium's closed-circuit monitors.

Wayne joined the taxidermists later that night as work began on the mount. No one except the taxidermists and select camera people knew the head was being worked on that night because I wanted the rack's location to be kept secret.

David Blanton, of Realtree Outdoors, and Wayne were careful not to interfere with each other's camera angles. They told me later that the whole evening went smoothly.

About 10 days later, with temperatures at minus 40, the group met again to record the taxidermists' finishing touches, including airbrushing the eyes and lips. Wayne and Rod took advantage of the miniature studio that Ian had set up in our living room for the portrait work. They shot a variety of backgrounds and lighting situations, and created some good effects by moving the spotlights and fading the lights in and out.

By that time, Wayne and Rod had accumulated a lot of material on the buck. In late January, the three of us edited a 12-minute production to take to the Saskatchewan Wildlife Federation's banquet in Biggar. Those who wanted to see pictures of the pending world-record buck were not disappointed. For the 60th Annual Saskatchewan Wildlife Convention, Wayne brought an expanded version of the video because the head was not available. The Hanson Buck video was a hit with sportsmen from all over Saskatchewan.

On Feb. 23, Wayne, Ian and I traveled to Precision Taxidermy in Briercrest. The Hanson Buck was to be permanently placed in a specially built display case made by Bub's friend, Brad Guillaume. Bub's shop became the center of attention, with plenty of free advice from onlookers. Bub and I decided to make a padded protective nylon cover for the display case.

A video on the history of the Hanson Buck was scheduled to be available to the public in late 1995. For information, write: YMVA; Box 04; Biggar, Saskatchewan, Canada S0K 0M0.

Ian McMurchy seemed to be one of the last people in the province to hear about the Hanson Buck. He was in bed with a nasty flu during deer season, which kept him out of touch. When he returned to work, everyone was talking about the huge whitetail they had seen on a recent news broadcast. Ian's director called him into his office to ask what he had heard about the new world-record deer. The question caught Ian flat-footed because he hadn't watched TV or listened to a radio for days. He didn't know anything about the deer or the hunter who shot it.

Ian was told a copy of the newscast was on its way to the office. He was asked to get in touch with me and arrange a meeting as quickly as possible. His task was to ensure I knew the provincial legalities about traveling with a trophy whitetail or selling one. Ian was also asked to arrange a photograph the province could use for promotions. In addition, he was told to provide any reasonable assistance, including possible storage of the head.

After contacting me, Ian prepared for our meeting, and looked forward to learning more about the buck. He said later that he was also concerned about the potential for conflict of interest because he had initiated contact on government time. He was aware of the photographic opportunities, and wanted to explore them, but he first had to fulfill his agency obligations. Even though he had now seen the TV interview of me with the buck, Ian didn't know what he was getting into.

Ian arrived at our farm at dusk on Dec. 9. We visited in my kitchen, and listened as the answering machine took all the phone calls. Ian reviewed the provincial laws about big-game trophies, and then we talked in detail about the outdoor magazine industry. Ian showed Olive and me his portfolio of magazine covers, which proved he knew something about the various publications and the white-tailed deer industry. We asked questions and listened attentively because Ian was the first person with magazine contacts who put our interests first.

When Ian returned home the next day, everyone at his office asked if he had seen the buck. Actually, we hardly talked about the head itself during that first visit, and it wasn't even on our property at the time. It was in a vault, and Ian said later he didn't know if he would ever get to see it himself. Ian and I kept in touch in the weeks that followed, and one evening I called him to clarify some issues about art and photography. I was slightly exasperated with all the various requests and demands for photos, and so I asked Ian if he would do the necessary photography. He said he wanted to pursue this opportunity, and suggested a meeting in Saskatoon to review our photography requirements and clarify his concern about conflict of interest.

During our discussions, we broke the photographic needs into three jobs: the scoring ceremony, the taxidermy work, and portraits for magazines and promotional publications. In addition, Ian identified several other photographic requirements, such as photos of the hunting party, my family, and logo material.

Ian and I assumed the portrait session could be done in my double garage, so he booked the suitable backdrops and a studio lighting system. He was confident in his ability to photograph the scoring ceremony and taxidermy work, but the studio work would be a new challenge. Still, he had worked before with studio lights, and was confident he could create unique lighting situations.

He started the photography at Bub Hill's studio as Bub and his wife, Myrna, worked on the head form and stretched the cape into place. Then Ian traveled to Biggar and shot about 350 photos of the scoring ceremony. The scoring itself happened quickly, and Ian had to be prepared to catch those one-time situations as they occurred. Ian used two Nikon F90 bodies with 35-to-70 and 80-to-200 auto-focus lenses and SB-25 flashes. All of his photographs were taken with Kodachrome 64 slide film, except for a few rolls of color prints.

Unlike some people at the ceremony, Ian noticed that I was nervous much of the time, and some of his photos captured that tension. Still, he said he was amazed how calmly I handled the event.

When the taxidermy work began, Bub took over. All of the cameramen just made sure they stayed out of his way. Bub knew what to do, and what to expect at every stage of the work. Even so, he was patient with the photographers and allowed them to shoot every angle and photo they wanted.

Ian found that the best location for the still-photography was atop a huge bag of sunflower seeds that supply Olive's bird feeders. The bag was in the front and center to the action, and just the right distance for his short zoom lens. Ian shot several photos from a few other angles, but spent most of his time shooting from atop the sunflower bag. Before the night was over, Ian had shot more than 300 frames of the taxidermy work.

Ian said later that watching the taxidermy work made for an incredible evening. He said he felt privileged to watch as Bub Hill turned the Hanson Buck into a piece of art. Everyone was amazed at the "presence" the antlers developed as the taxidermy work progressed. No one seemed prepared for the increasing awe they felt for this buck.

After the mount dried for a couple of weeks, everyone returned to watch Bub do the final touches. The buck seemed to come alive as Bub brushed and painted.

Then the onus was transferred to Ian as he worked on the portrait photos. He felt added pressure because magazines were waiting for pictures! We set up the backdrops and Ian prepared his cameras and lights. Then the reality of the garage's limitations hit us hard. The finished mount was just too big for the short-walled garage. We tried to vary the setup, but there was not enough room around the mount for a portrait photo. The garage ceiling was too low. Ian explained that magazine editors require certain compositions for cover photos and two-page spreads, and we simply lacked the necessary room for such formats.

We had no choice but to find another location. I preferred the security of my home, and didn't want to take the head to a studio or larger building. Fortunately, our home is a front-to-back split-level with an open two-story living room. We built a huge frame for a backdrop in the living room, essentially a false wall between there and the kitchen. It could now accommodate the oversize backdrops and the necessary lighting systems. Even so, we soon learned that even a 10-square-foot backdrop was not large enough when I posed beside the buck's mounted head! We had to go to 12-square-foot backdrops for my portrait with the buck. These were just big enough.

We often worked on the photography into the wee hours of the morning. I wanted to get the mount out of my house and back into the vault, so I urged Ian to finish his work. For the final shoot, which lasted three days, Ian asked Olive and me to block off all daylight coming into our kitchen and living room. We darkened the windows, and pretty much went without sunlight in our home for three days!

Frequently, video cameramen shared Ian's "studio" because various programs were prepared for local and international audiences.

At one point we tried shooting some portraits outdoors by using the huge door of my shop as a background. This proved impossible because it was minus 30 degrees. Nearly everyone froze, except for the mounted buck. Bub and I tried to look natural in light jackets or shirts, but even though Ian liked the late-afternoon light, we looked very uncomfortable in the photos! Plus, we had to work around some difficult shadows, which proved challenging even for Ian.

It was during these photo sessions that I realized Ian is a perfectionist. He did not want to just photograph the Hanson Buck; he wanted to shoot extraordinary photos. But there are only so many ways to photograph a buck's head. We tried a lot of lighting configurations, and Ian even back-lighted the rack with varying amounts of diffusion. We created some unique situations, and even Ian said some of the photos were pleasant surprises.

Throughout the photo sessions, I never let down my guard for the buck, and Bub often helped ensure the mount was secure. He and I pitched in to help Ian solve every problem he encountered. During all the shoots, the Hanson Buck was bolted to a large taxidermy pedestal. Bub had designed the mount to be free standing, not hang from a wall. That meant we had to find ways to support the head independently, yet keep the supporting pedestal hidden from view. We did this by cutting holes through the backdrops to keep the mount on one side of the cloth and the supporting pedestal on the other side.

We used a variety of background colors for the portraits. Black, blue and beige worked well, but Ian thought the yellows, oranges and reds were nothing special. Bub loaned bolts of taxidermy felt because we had to improvise on the backdrops. We had problems with seams and edges, but the biggest surprise was the amount of light absorbed by the dark felt. Dark felt acts as a light sponge. Even with powerful lights at close range Ian had few options for lens apertures. Eventually, Ian got the photos we needed, and the pictures have been published in many magazines.

After completing the main shoots, Ian also photographed the Hanson Buck as it was mounted in its custom-made oak display case. He also took some candid photos of me and the buck at some of the shows we attended.

The fellows involved have been fun to work with, and their video and color photos have done the buck justice.

Chapter 13

Art, Taxidermy and the Hanson Buck

Whenever I display the Hanson Buck, most people are riveted by its huge, symmetrical antlers. They tend to take for granted the taxidermy work on its cape, mouth, nose, ears and eyes. But not everyone overlooks these details. Some admirers critically examine every last inch of the mount, and often ask who did the taxidermy work. Everyone who sees the mount agrees this work is magnificent.

Therefore, I'm devoting this chapter to the taxidermist who turned this buck into a work of art. Bub Hill runs a taxidermy and archery-supply business in Briercrest, a small town several hours south of Biggar. Bub began working as a professional taxidermist in the late 1970s. His artwork reflects his deep interest in the outdoors and hunting. He knows wildlife, and he is a perfectionist who is only satisfied with the best work possible.

Taxidermist Bub Hill thought the Hanson Buck should be displayed on a pedestal mount that would allow it to be viewed from all sides when mounted inside a display case.

Bub first heard about the Hanson Buck in early December 1993 when an acquaintance called to say a new world-record deer had been shot in northern Saskatchewan. Because he is a professional taxidermist, Bub had heard similar tales in the past, and they all turned out to be false.

"But this time it sounded different," Bub said. "One night the local TV station announced it would have a report about the buck on its 6 o'clock news. Like thousands of other Saskatchewan hunters, I watched to see if the story was true. Sure enough, there was a picture of Milo Hanson holding the biggest white-tailed deer I had ever seen. The score they gave was 214-4/8 Boone and Crockett typical points."

Naturally, because Bub's profession is taxidermy, he was curious about who would mount the deer. He wrote down my name with the intention of phoning the next day. However, Bub said he gave this idea a lot of thought, assumed I was already getting too many phone calls, and decided he wouldn't bother me.

"I threw the piece of paper with Milo's name in the garbage, and went about my business," he said.

Two days after watching the news story, Bub drove to

People are riveted by the Hanson Buck's huge, symmetrical antlers. They tend to take for granted the taxidermy work on its cape, mouth, nose, ears and eyes. However, knowledgeable observers agree the taxidermy is magnificent.

89

Regina to attend a meeting with Dennis Sherratt, the director of Saskatchewan's wildlife branch. The Hanson Buck came up during their conversation, and Sherratt told Bub that Ian McMurchy was traveling to Biggar the next morning to meet with me on behalf of the wildlife branch. Ian and Bub had worked together on several archery-related photo sessions, and Ian was familiar with Bub's work. Bub learned later that Ian had suggested his name to me during one of our early meetings.

One day I called Bub to ask if he would mount the buck. We set a date to visit his studio, view some of his mounts, and possibly work out arrangements for mounting the deer. I brought along Al Ashkar, an amateur taxidermist from Biggar. After looking over Bub's impressive displays, Bub and I agreed he would take on the Hanson Buck, and that Al would assist him. I left the caped-out hide with Bub that afternoon.

Bub made two requests. The first was that he could work on the deer somewhere other than his shop. He did not want the responsibility of having the rack in his possession for an extended time. I readily agreed because I did not want the rack out of my sight for long. Bub's second request was that no one be told he was mounting the deer until the work was finished. If the public believed the rack was in his possession, the effect would be the same as having the rack itself. He didn't need that hassle! I agreed to keep his identity secret, and we then worked out details on how and when the deer would be mounted.

Before I left that day, Bub said the hunting portion of my life would now take place in a fish bowl. He also expressed hope that outside pressures from people wanting to exploit the buck would not cause me to regret the day I made the accomplishment public.

Although Bub agreed to mount the buck, we hadn't determined what type of mount we would use to best display its enormous rack. After much thought, Bub came up with the idea of a pedestal mount that would allow the buck to be viewed from all sides when mounted in a glass display case. He drew a few sketches of his ideas and presented them to me during a meeting with Ian in Saskatoon. I approved the basic concept, and Bub agreed to find someone to build the mount's base and display case.

Bub's next step was to begin tanning the deer's cape in preparation for mounting. His first impression was that the cape was not in good shape. The field-dressing incision ran the entire length of the brisket and 4 inches into the neck. Also, its hair had been marked by barbwire, the line starting between the buck's eyes, and then running over its right eye and down across the right shoulder. While the hide itself was only slightly pierced by the wire in two places, hair had been cut the entire length, leaving a mark that was impossible to cover. An entrance hole from a bullet also marred the right shoulder. A lot of hair around the wound had been cut off by the impact. In addition, when the buck was caped, a dorsal cut had been made the full length of the neck, which would be hard to disguise. Finally, there was the shot to the head that entered behind the right ear. The bullet damaged the hide for 4 inches, traveled under the hide at the back of the skull, and exited through the left ear. Fortunately, the bullet did not damage the skull plate, but it would require a lot of repair to produce a quality mount.

With all of the damage to the hide, Bub offered the option of using a different cape on the mount. That is nothing unusual under such circumstances. But because this was the potential world-record buck, I wanted to have it mounted with the original cape if possible.

After tanning the hide, Bub began working to repair and conceal the hide's imperfections. He cut away the hide with damaged hair around the bullet holes, and about a 5-inch section of the wire cut along the right shoulder. Then, using a series of blind stitches, he began the tedious task of closing the wire cut, the bullet holes, about 6 inches of the lower neck and brisket, and the back of the neck from the skull's base to the withers. He didn't keep track of how much time these procedures required, but it was likely five or six hours. Bub used epoxy to rebuild the portion of the left ear that was destroyed by the killing shot.

"Although these repairs required extra work, by the time I finished the mount, I knew Milo was right to retain the original cape," Bub said. "The wire mark adds character to the deer and, as you can see in the photos, the rest of its cape is beautiful."

Bub and I decided to mount the buck on a form that had a slight right turn. This would better display the antlers' two small non-typical points. Because Bub had not seen the animal before it was caped, he could only take measurements from the hide to determine what size form was required. He brought in two sizes of forms to be sure the cape would fit properly. He ordered the forms from Knapton's Studios in Ontario.

Once Bub determined which form to use, he began the alterations needed for a pedestal mount. The fact that this buck might be shipped around the country for display also meant the base and display case had to be built to withstand rough handling. Its design includes a large metal plate that is attached to the back of the mount. This then connects at a 90-degree angle to another plate that is bolted to the display case's floor.

All of the above work was done before Bub ever saw the antlers. In fact, it wasn't until after the official scoring was completed Jan. 22, 1994, that Bub ever touched the rack. He wanted to do as much work as possible beforehand in his studio, where he had access to all his tools. His intent was to mount the cape on the form, complete a large portion of the taxidermy work, and attach the form to the base Jan. 21, the day before he went to Biggar. Doing half of a mount one day and completing it the next was something Bub had never tried before. Therefore, he did a couple of practice runs on other deer in his studio, and was pleased with the results.

In the meantime, the base was built by Brad Guillaume, a superb carpenter from Marquis, Saskatchewan. Guillaume is also a fanatical hunter, and Bub knew he would appreciate the importance of this job. Clint Sandborn of Moose Jaw helped design and build the metal components of the base. Bub gave these components to Brad, along with a sketch of what he wanted for the beautiful oak base.

On the evening of Jan. 21, with Ian present to photograph the process, Bub began the preparatory work on the actual mounting of the buck. The next night, after the buck was taken from the scoring ceremony to my farm, Bub completed his work.

He proceeded carefully at every step. When I shot the buck, a piece of one of my bullets lodged in the back of the right antler about 6 inches up from the base. Before mounting the head, Bub reinforced the damaged area of the antler with black electrician's tape.

"I had no desire to gain notoriety as the taxidermist responsible for destroying the potential world-record white-tail," Bub said. "After all, Milo had made arrangements to have the mounting filmed for a TV show, and there were two other photographers there to record the event on video and in photos."

Bub still recalls the first time he saw the buck's rack.

"The antlers of this enormous deer were lying on a table waiting to be scored at the ceremony," he said. "I admit I was not overly impressed. But after they were mounted and I had something tangible to help put the rack into perspective, all that changed."

After the basic taxidermy work was finished, Bub and the photographers spent the next hour sitting across the room in complete fascination. This was obviously the most impressive whitetail they had ever seen.

Bub spent the next couple of days in our home as he made minor alterations to the mount during the initial drying stages. He then drove home, but returned two weeks later to do the finishing and painting of the deer. The next step was to install the mount in its display case. The case was designed as a fine piece of furniture. Brad, with the help of Aaron Hill and Doug Kunts, had searched several lumber yards for the best pieces of oak they could find. Using this oak and Plexiglas, they designed and built a beautiful case that has an internal lighting system complete with UV filters to prevent the buck's hair from fading. Despite its delicate look, the case can withstand rough and frequent handling.

One evening in February, we drove to Bub's shop to begin the actual installation. While Brad and the others worked to install the Plexiglas and attach the mount's base to the case's floor, Bub finished sewing a padded nylon cover that fully encloses the case for handling and shipping.

The hour was very late when we had everything complete. A bad Saskatchewan blizzard had settled in as we worked that night, reducing visibility to near zero and closing the major highways. Almost everyone spent the night at Bub's house. Two of the guys even slept on the floor of his shop. After breakfast the next day, we carried the mount and oak case — now enclosed in the nylon cover — out the shop's back door, dragged it across more than 3 feet of snow, and loaded it into the back of my truck. This provided a good test for the unit's durability, and everything stood up well. The buck's next destination was a storage vault in Regina.

Bub said he enjoyed his work on the Hanson Buck.

"In a small way I crawled into Milo's fish bowl, and it was a pleasant and rewarding experience," he said. "If this mount is scheduled to appear anywhere near your home, I encourage you to see its awesome antlers, and meet the man who shot the biggest typical whitetail ever recorded."

Chapter 14

Fame, Recognition and Publicity

Having the world-record whitetail consumes part of every day for me. The amount varies from all day to just a few thoughts on busy farming days. Although it's been a struggle at times, I've become comfortable being the hunter who has the record. I don't think the instant fame changed me much as a person, but it certainly changed parts of my life.

I am amazed how far the story of the Hanson Buck has spread. For instance, when a friend traveled to Germany recently, some hunters asked where he was from. When he said Saskatchewan, they started talking about the Hanson Buck. They even showed magazine pictures they had accumulated.

That might be an unusual circumstance, but there's no doubt shooting the Hanson Buck brought me instant celebrity status among hunters in Canada and the United States,

Having the world's record whitetail consumes part of almost every day for Milo Hanson.

whether I liked it or not. All I know is that I never imagined receiving such attention when I shot this buck on that late-November day in 1993.

And there is little a person can do to prepare for the publicity crunch. Although I once had jobs that involved dealing daily with the public, I had little or no experience during the previous 20 years with public speaking, or greeting and meeting strangers. During those years, Olive and I were busy running the farm, and we mainly socialized with neighbors. Everyone knows me as a fairly quiet person who is not exceptionally outgoing.

I'll always remember how nervous I was during the first interviews and speeches. That gradually changed during 1994 as I was interviewed dozens of times for newspapers and magazine articles, and radio and TV broadcasts. I have also become more comfortable giving speeches or talks, although I still get a bit nervous.

We have taken the Hanson Buck's mount to sport shows attended by tens of thousands of hunters and their families. These experiences have made me more comfortable with meeting people and signing autographs. I enjoy this aspect of my new life because I never get tired of meeting folks one on one, and I particularly enjoy hearing about their lives and their deer hunting. Ian McMurchy has attended some of the shows with me, and he jokes that I am becoming an expert at "doing shows."

Most people are just plain friendly toward me. I get asked a few questions repeatedly, such as: "So, what's it like to have the big one?"; "Do you still enjoy hunting?"; "What is the tape on the antler for?"; and "What are you going to do with the buck?" Many of these hunters have an amazing knowledge about me and the Hanson Buck. They have saved every magazine with any mention of the buck. I am often easily recognized at deer shows and elsewhere, and at times I get self-conscious when people treat me as a celebrity. In Biggar the recognition factor is high, and I hear deer stories start up

Besides hearing from people by telephone and letters, Milo and Olive also make personal appearances at shows. Here, they talk to well-wishers at Bass Pro Shops.

wherever I am. Obviously, deer hunting is something I have in common with many people, so it gives us a reference point for conversation.

Besides attending shows in cities far from home, I've gone to a couple in Biggar and my hometown in southwestern Saskatchewan. I found these shows more stressful because I knew so many people, and didn't have time to have a good talk with them.

Naturally, my heart and interests are largely with the Biggar area. Everyone in Biggar had heard about my buck, so no one was surprised when I won the Biggar Wildlife Federation's trophy for "Best Typical Whitetail" and also the "Best Overall Big Game Head" in 1993. More than 350 people attended the awards banquet. I was especially pleased when the wildlife club honored my hunting partners with plaques recognizing their "World Record Hunting Trip." Walter Meger, Rene Igini and John Yaroshko were surprised and happy to get special souvenirs of our hunt.

Olive and I also attended the annual Saskatchewan Wildlife Federation convention in Yorkton. Several hundred delegates from throughout the province met for three days to discuss wildlife and fisheries issues. On Feb. 17, 1994, the group presented me the Saskatchewan Wildlife Federation's Henry Kelsey Club award for "Best Typical Whitetail" with a green score of 214-4/8. In addition, I received the "Ernie Paynter Trophy" for "Best Overall Big Game Head Taken in 1993." I was humbled, yet proud to receive these trophies.

Ian also arranged for the provincial wildlife federation to obtain 100 8-by-10-inch color photographs of my buck with the provincial flag in the background. The federation sold these photos as a fund-raiser for the habitat program. Some of these prints later sold at other fund-raising banquets for as much as $100! I was pleased to autograph the photos and make a small contribution toward protecting wildlife habitat for Saskatchewan's future.

Besides making personal appearances and meeting new people at shows, I also hear from many folks by telephone and mail. One of the nicest aspects of having the world-record whitetail is receiving letters from deer hunters throughout Canada and the United States. I get calls from many hunters who just want to congratulate me, and then talk hunting for a while. At times the calls became an avalanche, however, and started to get me down. That was because I had too many more pressing demands on my time. After all, Olive and I still have our lives and a farm to run.

I try to reply to virtually every letter I receive. Some fellows have even written back, and I can follow how their hunting seasons have gone. I enjoy seeing pictures of their bucks, and I study the type of country they hunt. We also compare guns, weather, farming operations and all kinds of topics.

Some folks have even driven out to our farm to visit, but

that seldom works out well for us or them. We are always busy with the farm operation. Anyone who has ever farmed knows what I mean. Also, I don't keep the Hanson Buck's mount here very often, so visitors are disappointed when I tell them I can't show it to them.

I'm happy to say I have not encountered much animosity, ill will or jealousy at home or on the road. I have heard the odd comment from someone who looks at the buck and asks loudly what all of the fuss is about, and a few hunters have told me they've shot much bigger bucks than mine, but such behavior is fairly rare. I received a couple of letters from anti-hunters that totally puzzled me. Their comments made me wonder what makes some people tick.

Still, when considering all of the new people I have met since I shot the buck, I have not had one truly negative experience. Most of the letters, calls and visits have come from people much like Olive and me. I guess their collective good will doesn't totally surprise me. Hunters, after all, tend to be friendly people.

Chapter 15

The Business Side of the Hanson Buck

Many people ask if Olive and I have made a fortune off the world record. I don't deny we have gained significantly, and I am aware we could make a lot more money by "working" the buck. But we do not intend to make marketing the Hanson Buck our life's profession or primary goal. At this time we don't intend to go on a regular road circuit or do a lot of traveling with the buck. We've learned to always proceed carefully. We consider and discuss all offers that come in, and then determine where we can get the best return for our time and effort.

I have not set a price on the Hanson Buck's mount. And yes, I have had a couple of actual offers to buy the mount, but I turned them down. Also, most of the continent's biggest antler collectors have contacted me to let me know they are interested in buying the head if I should ever consider it. What is the mount's value? Everyone has a different opinion. All I know is the buck is invaluable to me, and that he's not for sale.

I'm always amazed at the incredible number of stories and rumors about me and the Hanson Buck. Most tales involve the many millions of dollars I am supposedly making from the buck, or that the buck itself is being sold in some immense transaction somewhere. Depending on whom you talk with, I've been wheeling and dealing with British breweries, major truck companies, firearms and camo companies, and anyone else you care to name. Either that or everyone who's anyone has made an offer to buy the head within the past few weeks. Olive and I get a kick out of the stories, and we wish some of them were true! After all, farming can be a risky business.

While such stories are humorous, I have learned that the business side of a world record is a serious matter. When I first met Ian McMurchy he told me of the wide range of commercial opportunities that would develop.

Of course, even before Ian made his comments, we were becoming aware of the commercial possibilities. We had heard from a variety of promoters and media people. Ian informed us of the many publication, copyright and promotional rights that accompanied the shooting of a world-class buck. We did not know such rights existed until then, so we quickly became careful about protecting our rights to ensure we weren't exploited.

I'll list some of the rights every hunter should be aware of when shooting a large buck, but space doesn't allow me to describe all the details of each.

* Story rights: You can negotiate publication rights with books and magazines. A publisher could seek anything from one-time publication rights to perpetual rights.

* Photo rights: Once you shoot the buck and legally take possession, you can claim rights to all photos from the

time it's shot until its mount is on your wall.

    * Art rights: These rights include originals and prints of paintings, drawings and sketches.

    * TV production rights.

    * Video production rights.

    * Product-endorsement rights.

Needless to say, these are not black-and-white issues. Be advised that you must not confuse rights with marketing potential. You might make demands that no publisher, producer or manufacturer deems worth the cost. On the other hand, be vigilant to ensure no one profits from your deer without your consent.

In addition to the rights above, I've found there are many commercial opportunities to consider. These include:

    * Displaying the head at shows.

    * Selling reproductions of the antlers.

    * Selling commemorative material such as posters, buckles, caps, T-shirts, etc.

Olive and I set up a proprietorship company to handle the Hanson Buck business opportunities. We also decided to protect the name "The Hanson Buck" so we could control the commercial use of our name. This involved meetings with our lawyers, which meant a good deal of time and expense.

Since the Hanson Buck became publicized, I have noticed that many deer logos on caps and advertisements have become wide-racked 12-pointers. Perhaps the Hanson Buck has become a trend-setter for deer images. Most of these images of a 12-point buck are not direct copies of the Hanson Buck, but some are extremely similar in appearance to it. In fact, we have become aware of a couple of copyright infringements on the buck's image, and we have had to take legal action.

Another business decision was how to insure the head. As you might expect, this required a lot of time and effort because our insurance agent had never encountered such a request before. He needed information that included the mount's immediate and potential value, and few authorities are qualified to make such estimates.

We have taken the buck to some deer shows, and plan to do more in the future as time permits. I'll always remember the first time we took the Hanson Buck to a show in the United States. Two businessmen had flown to Saskatoon to negotiate a deal to feature the buck at a new show they were promoting in Florence, S.C. I was concerned about traveling with the Hanson Buck, but the fellows offered to haul the mount in a custom-made aluminum case in a contracted semi-trailer. They were good to their word, and the Hanson Buck was hauled 2,500 miles to South Carolina in an air-ride equipped semi-trailer.

Ian and I rode to the show with a relative of one of the organizers. The trip was wonderful, but we had some interesting times when crossing the United States/Canadian border. We had difficulty convincing border officials that the semi-trailer was hauling one deer head and nothing but one deer head!

We also took the buck to Bass Pro Shops in Springfield, Mo., as a feature for one of its big hunting shows in summer 1994. Some hunters drove more than 800 miles to see the buck. We were not accustomed to Missouri's heat nor the tremendous crowd size, but we had a good time. It was at this show that Ian and I introduced our 18-by-24-inch poster of the Hanson Buck.

Another common question I hear is if the mount on display is the original or a replica. We did not have time to get a mold made of the rack before the taxidermy work was done. Therefore, as of 1995, no replicas of the Hanson Buck have been cast. However, Bub Hill is interested in making replicas, and we plan to explore the possibilities.

Chapter 16

One Year Later: The '94 Hunting Season

As the 1994 hunting season approached, many people asked how I would handle this deer season after having shot a world-record in 1993. All I knew was that I love hunting, and nothing had changed as far as my anticipation of going out and enjoying the sport.

One easily seen change for 1994 — although it had nothing to do with the Hanson Buck — was that I took up muzzle-loading deer hunting in 1994. I decided to try it at the urging of Ian McMurchy. I bought a beautiful stainless steel .50-caliber Knight MK-85, and mounted a 3-9X Redfield scope with Warne detachable rings. I then sighted in with 310-grain saboted bullets. I was impressed how well this rifle shot out to 150 yards. Walter Meger also bought a Knight rifle, and we started hunting in October during the province's special muzzle-loading season. We didn't get any shots, but we had a

105

New year, new rifle. Milo proudly displays his Winchester Model 70 bolt-action .30-06, which he first used during the 1994 deer season.

lot of fun trying to find bucks to stalk. Some big muleys live in our area, but we never found them during this early season. We definitely got the muzzle-loading bug, and it's now part of our annual hunting plans.

One morning during the special muzzle-loading season for whitetails, I was out with the new Knight rifle when I came across a car containing a couple of hunters. As I slowed down to talk to them, one of the fellows recognized me and jumped out of the vehicle. He said he recognized me from magazine articles, and he wanted to meet me. The hunters, Peter Rogal and George Evanoff, said they were in our area looking for big whitetails. I knew George because he farms near Biggar. He introduced me to Peter and we had a good visit. In November, Walter, Gerry Yaroshko and I ended up hunting moose with Peter at his farm near Meadow Lake, about two hours north of our farm.

We also hunted antelope in southern Saskatchewan, and then got ready for the mule deer rifle season. When that season began, I shot the first buck I saw, much to Olive's surprise. She even yelled that I shouldn't shoot because it was small, but I wanted to fill my tag. I got a bit of static from my buddies about not having the whitetail and mule deer records! I enjoyed this hunt, and was proud when Olive brought in the big muley buck everyone had been hunting all season. Olive's buck gross-scored 200-3/8 and netted 182-1/8. The antlers have good mass and long forks, but several non-typical sticker points added up to 12-3/8 inches in deductions.

During the mule deer season, my old Winchester 88 lever-action rifle started to misfire. As a matter of fact, the first shot I fired after killing the Hanson Buck was a misfire. If that rifle had misfired a couple of rounds earlier, the Hanson Buck might have gotten another name!

I didn't want to hunt with a rifle I couldn't trust, so I went to Saskatoon and bought a Winchester Model 70 bolt-action with a detachable magazine. This new rifle is in .30-06 and carries a 3-9X Redfield scope.

By the time our white-tailed deer rifle season came around, we knew of some good bucks in our area but no monster like the year before. We hunted our regular areas the first day and saw some big bucks, but didn't shoot at anything. I also tried something new for me that autumn: rattling antlers. I walked into a good area, rattled for a few minutes, and brought in a little buck. I found rattling to be exciting and satisfying. The next day I tried rattling for a while in the morning. I could hear a buck coming in, and his rack hit a branch, but he must have winded me. All of a sudden he stopped, and I never heard or saw anything more. My rifle was up and ready, but he had beaten me.

I went into town that morning to buy some supplies for a moose hunt and some salt blocks for our cattle. On the way

How do you follow up the world's No. 1 buck? Shoot another record-class animal. Milo displays his 1994 firearms kill, a 170-class buck.

back I dropped off some blocks in my pasture. As I was driving out, I saw two white-tailed fawns standing in a big slough. I got out of the truck and blew my grunt tube and a bleat call. The fawns listened intently and walked a few steps closer. Then a big doe stood up, and I again blew the calls.

Suddenly, 50 feet from the other deer, a good buck jumped up and ran into a rolling brushy area nearby. The other deer followed. I couldn't get a shot, so I walked back to the truck, drove to the end of the pasture, and then walked a quarter of a mile to the end of the slough in the direction they were heading. I soon heard deer approaching through brush along the slough's edge. The doe and fawns came into sight, and

World-record buck or not, the hunt is still the most important aspect for Milo. In fact, he took up rattling and calling in 1994.

then the big buck followed as the group ran across in front of me. I shouldered my new rifle and fired as he ran slightly away from me at about 125 yards.

The 150-grain bullet hit him in the neck, killing him instantly. I checked him over, and then walked back for the truck. He's an impressive 12-point buck, scoring more than 170 points. I guess I'm the only hunter whose smaller entry in the record books will be 40 points lower than his biggest buck.

My 1994 buck even won the Biggar Big Buck contest, which was my second such honor in two years.

I had other offers to hunt in autumn 1994, including trips to the Southern United States, but I'm reluctant to leave the farm for that long.

No doubt 1993 was an incredible year for me, but we had a lot of fun in 1994. My hope is that I'll have just as much fun in the years to come.

Chapter 17

It's Official: The Hanson Buck is No. 1

Ever since the 60-day scoring ceremony took place in Biggar on Jan. 22, 1994, I thought about the day when the Hanson Buck would be panel-scored and accepted as the world-record typical white-tailed deer. Those doubts and anxieties hung over my head for almost 18 months. The final trips to Dallas, Texas, for the official Boone & Crockett Club's scoring sessions and induction ceremony were the final hurdles. Some would say these two events were mere formalities, but for me they were big steps to take before I could accept the reality of having the world-record deer.

On April 24, 1995, I began these final journeys. After loading the buck into my special travel vehicle, I drove down to Regina to pick up Ian McMurchy, and then we drove to Dallas. Ian accompanied me to help drive and navigate, and to shoot some photographs of the panel scoring.

111

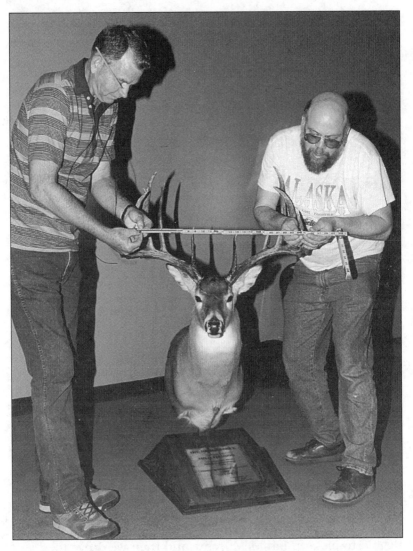

Jimmy Engelman of Arizona and Ron Boucher of Vermont were the first scorers to work on the Hanson Buck in Dallas.

Along the way we stopped to visit the Cabela's outdoors retail store in Sidney, Neb., which we enjoyed greatly. We arrived in Dallas at the Boone & Crockett Club's assembly site on the morning of April 26. All of the trophies for the induction were to be delivered to the Dallas Museum of Natural History the next day. We dropped off the Hanson Buck the next morning, and then assisted the Boone & Crockett folks in handling some of the magnificent trophies that were submitted. What a sight! We helped move many of the finest moose, elk, caribou, musk oxen, mule deer, sheep, bear and antelope trophies ever taken.

For me, perhaps one of the most memorable trophies was a certain 8-by-8 bull elk, the last large head mount to be taken into the museum. I'll explain why: We helped move the trophies to a large room on the museum's second floor. To get there, we frequently used a freight elevator for the heaviest heads. Ian and I carried the huge elk up a flight of stairs into the building, and then we carefully placed it into the elevator. I was backed into a corner by the size of the giant rack, and Ian was wedged into the opposite corner, near the control panel.

Ian pushed the button for the second floor, and the door closed and we slowly started going up. Shortly after, the elevator bumped a couple of times, made a few groaning noises, and then stopped. Ian hit the button to open the door, but no luck. Next he hit almost every button on the panel, but still no luck. Then he reluctantly hit the warning button, which sounded a loud buzzer. Soon after, a lady's voice told us to hang on a minute. She said she would try something, and that she would get us out shortly.

Thirty or 40 minutes later, we were still stuck in the elevator. The lady told us a repairman was on his way. Somehow, that didn't reassure us because we didn't know how far he had to travel to reach us. The air inside the elevator was getting quite warm, and Ian started to feel a little claustrophobic. He told me that we had better get his mind off of this mess, so we joked about a variety of things, including the thought of prying the door open with the huge tines of the 8-point elk! Ian kept his cool, and eventually the lady tried one last thing. The elevator responded with a lurch, and the door opened.

The floor wasn't lined up properly, but we wasted little time getting ourselves and the elk out into the hallway. After that experience, Ian didn't like getting into an elevator with me, but he slowly regained his trust.

The next day — with the help of Ian and Ron Boucher, a Boone and Crockett scorer from Vermont — I removed the Hanson Buck from its display case to prepare for the panel scoring. Ron is a skilled carpenter and cabinetmaker, and understood the intricate process of removing the mount from the custom-made display case. I then showed Ron the tricks involved in returning the mount to the case. Ron would be in charge of that job in a few days because Ian and I could not stay in Dallas until the three scoring panels were finished with the buck.

The Hanson Buck stayed in Ron's care during our absence. That was the first time the buck was out of my possession for an extended period, but I felt comfortable leaving Ron in charge. We had been in touch with each other since shortly after I shot the buck. The first time we had talked he had given me some sound advice: Only the Boone & Crockett Club could declare a new world record, and all the writers and magazine articles in the world didn't mean a thing until the club made the record official.

During my first trip to Dallas, Ron officially scored the buck I shot in 1994. Its final net score was 171-3/8, which will put it into the Boone & Crockett Club's record book. Ron believes I was the first hunter to shoot Boone & Crockett bucks two years in a row.

The next day, the Boone & Crockett judging panels began scoring the trophies in a large room adjacent to where the heads were stored. No one but Boone and Crockett scorers

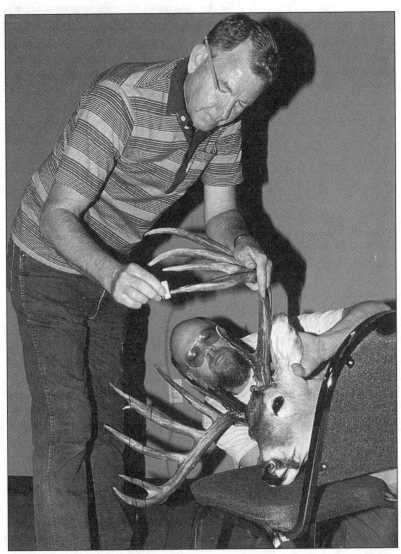

During the official scoring, the Hanson Buck's score increased one-half inch to 213-5/8 for entry into the record book.

and officials were allowed in the room during the scoring sessions. Ron Boucher and Jimmy Engelman of Arizona were the first team of scorers to work on the Hanson Buck. Shortly after Ron picked up a blank score sheet and prepared for the job, he said all hell broke loose in the room. Ron said practically everybody who was working in the room came over to look at the Hanson Buck. Everyone wanted to watch, take pictures and somehow get into the act.

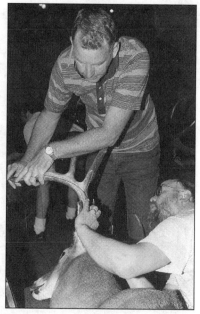

"A lot of talk and commotion was going on," Ron said. "We were all used to being around and measuring world-class and world-record trophies, but I don't mind telling you the Hanson Buck humbled us all! Finally, I told everybody

Ron Boucher, kneeling, said that scoring the Hanson Buck's rack was an incredibly emotional experience for him.

we had to get to work and to leave us alone."

Ron said that scoring the rack was an incredibly emotional experience for him.

"I remember feeling oblivious to all that surrounded me," he said. "I was trying to absorb the whole measuring experience. I knew it would be short-lived, and it was. When it was over, I watched Phil Wright (former chairman of the records committee) add up the measurements. The thought crossed my mind that it was done. For a few moments I actually almost felt depressed. The event I had anxiously awaited was ending."

Ron said later that the rack was simple to score.

"Our biggest concern was carefully positioning the head on a cushioned chair for measuring the beam length," he said. "We were very much aware of the fragile nature of the partially split beam. I told Jimmy to shoot me immediately if I did anything accidental to cause the beam to split! He said he understood."

Because no one except scorers and B&C officials were allowed in the room, Ian and I couldn't watch the scoring. Still, we wanted some photographic record of the event, so Ron and Jimmy kindly agreed to pose later for a re-enactment. Ron and Jimmy were sworn to secrecy about the score they had given the Hanson Buck. I couldn't help but wonder what was going through their heads as they re-enacted the first official scoring of the Hanson Buck.

That night Ron gave me the B&C tape measure they had used to measure the Hanson Buck. He couldn't tell me anything about the score, but he wanted me to have the tape measure as a gift and souvenir. It was brand new and had never been used before on any other head.

After shooting the re-enactment photos, Ian and I started the 30-hour drive home to Saskatchewan.

During the next few days, the Hanson Buck was measured by two more two-man panels. That was later followed by a meeting of the chairman, consultants and the measurers involved. They compared score sheets and the entry score. I learned later that practically all the scores were identical. The only slight differences were in the beam lengths. The panel members, as a group, remeasured the beams and reached a final decision for the beam lengths.

A couple weeks after our return, I received a call from the Boone & Crockett Club's headquarters. During the conversation, I was told the score had increased one-half inch to 213-5/8 for official entry into the record book. Shortly after, I received a letter and copy of the official score sheet in the mail. Amazingly enough, the inside spread did not change during any of the measurements. Much of the half-inch difference resulted from a rule change involving how the main beam should be measured. This measurement is now taken on the extreme outside of the beam, resulting in a slightly longer distance.

About one month later, on June 6, 1995, Ian and I again drove to Dallas. We immediately went to the Museum of Natural History, and spent several enjoyable hours looking at all of the Boone & Crockett trophies, which had been arranged into a spectacular display.

We also attended a social function at the museum, where we met many of the trophies' owners and Boone & Crockett Club members.

On June 10, we went to the Boone & Crockett Club's 22nd North American Big Game Awards luncheon. Several hundred people gathered to enjoy this recognition of the top big-game trophies taken from 1992 to 1994. I sat at a table with John Crouse, a young man from Cordova, Alaska, who shot the world record Alaska-Yukon moose. John and I were a little nervous, but the other men at the table kept us loose, allowing us to enjoy the meal and program.

I was talking to someone and didn't quite hear the master of ceremonies call the owners of the whitetail and Coues deer trophies to come up and receive our awards. John told me to get going! The time had finally come. I remember walking around the crowd, and being told to go to the front of the line. All of a sudden, I was walking to the front of the ballroom, and many camera flashes were going off. Randy Byers, the awards chairman, presented me with a certificate and a small box containing the gold Boone & Crockett Club medallion. Randy and I posed a few minutes for more photos, and then I returned to the table.

I opened the envelope with the beautiful Boone & Crockett certificate, and then examined the medallion. On its back is engraved: "First Award — 1995. T. Whitetail Deer 213 5/8, Milo N. Hanson."

After John received his awards for the moose, we compared

them like little kids. I shocked John by asking him to sign my banquet program. It was the first time he had ever been asked for an autograph. We had a fine afternoon. That evening we celebrated at a Dallas restaurant. The owner, Matt Martinez, treated our group as if we were celebrities. We enjoyed an incredible meal, not to mention many great stories.

The next morning, Ian and I reclaimed the Hanson Buck, reloaded it into my truck, and started the long trip home. I guess we were running on adrenalin and Matt's great food, because we drove straight through to Saskatchewan. We took turns napping and talking about the previous week. The trip had passed quickly.

I look back on the trips to Dallas as great experiences. Because I'm a farmer, I particularly enjoyed seeing the wide variety of agricultural practices throughout the journey. Ian said he noticed me checking out every crop, tractor, farm implement and cattle operation that we drove past. We also watched for wildlife, and we even marveled at road-kills such as opossums and armadillos because neither of us had ever seen such creatures before!

Most importantly, though, the trips to Dallas allowed us to meet many wonderful people and make some new friends. Those are pleasures that never would have been possible without the Hanson Buck.

The Hanson Buck: The 60-Day Score

Final Score: 213-1/8

The Stats:

Scorable Points: 14		**Abnormal Points:** 2-5/8	
Right Antler 8		Right Antler 1-2/8, 1-3/8	
Left Antler 6		**Greatest Spread:** 29-1/8	
Inside Spread: 27-2/8		**Tip-to-Tip Spread:** 24-4/8	

Area	Right	Left	Difference
Length of Main Beam	28-3/8	28-1/8	2/8
Length of First Point	6-6/8	6-0/8	6/8
Length of Second Point	12-3/8	13-0/8	5/8
Length of Third Point	13-6/8	14-0/8	2/8
Length of Fourth Point	11-4/8	11-6/8	2/8
Length of Fifth Point	5-0/8	7-1/8	2-1/8
Circumference Between Burr and First Point	4-6/8	5-0/8	2/8
Circumference Between First and Second Points	4-2/8	4-2/8	0/8
Circumference Between Second and Third Points	4-3/8	4-2/8	1/8
Circumference Between Third and Fourth Points	4-2/8	4-2/8	0/8
Totals	**95-3/8**	**97-6/8**	**7-2/8**

Exact Location of Kill: Seven miles north of Biggar, Saskatchewan, Canada **Taken by:** Milo Hanson, 11/23/93. **Measured by:** B. Allemand, A. Holtvogt and N. Parchewsky.	Spread: 27-2/8 Column 1: 95-3/8 Column 2: 97-6/8 **Subtotal: 220-3/8** minus difference: 7-2/8 minus abnormal: 2-5/8	Final Score: **213-1/8**

Milo's 1994 Boone & Crockett Buck

Final Score: 171-3/8

The Stats:

Scorable Points: 15		**Abnormal Points:** 10-4/8	
Right Antler 7		Right Antler 3-3/8	
Left Antler 8		Left Antler 2-7/8, 2-3/8, 1-7/8	
Inside Spread: 19-5/8		**Greatest Spread:** 23	
		Tip-to-Tip Spread: 7-3/8	

Area	Right	Left	Difference
Length of Main Beam	27-3/8	26-5/8	6/8
Length of First Point	7-3/8	7-2/8	1/8
Length of Second Point	13-1/8	11	2-1/8
Length of Third Point	10-3/8	10-6/8	3/8
Length of Fourth Point	8-1/8	8-7/8	6/8
Length of Fifth Point	1-4/8		1-4/8
Circumference Between Burr and First Point	4-7/8	4-7/8	
Circumference Between First and Second Points	4-4/8	4-3/8	1/8
Circumference Between Second and Third Points	4-4/8	4-3/8	1/8
Circumference Between Third and Fourth Points	4-1/8	4-2/8	1/8
Totals	**85-7/8**	**82-3/8**	**16-4/8**

Exact Location of Kill: Biggar, Saskatchewan, Canada **Taken by:** Milo Hanson on Nov. 16, 1994 **Measured by:** Ron Boucher	Spread: 19-5/8 Column 1: 85-7/8 Column 2: 82-3/8 **Subtotal:** **187-7/8** minus Column 4: 16-4/8 minus Abnormal: 10-4/8	Final Score: **171-3/8**

121

The Jordan Buck: The Previous Record

Final Score: 206-1/8

The Stats:

Scorable Points: 10   **Abnormal Points:** none
Right Antler 5   **Greatest Spread:** 23-6/8
Left Antler 5   **Tip-to-Tip Spread:** 7-5/8
Inside Spread: 20-1/8

Area	Right	Left	Difference
Length of Main Beam	30-0/8	30-0/8	0/8
Length of First Point	7-6/8	7-3/8	3/8
Length of Second Point	13-0/8	13-1/8	1/8
Length of Third Point	10-0/8	10-4/8	4/8
Length of Fourth Point	6-0/8	7-5/8	1-5/8
Length of Fifth Point	–	–	–
Circumference Between Burr and First Point	6-2/8	6-1/8	1/8
Circumference Between First and Second Points	6-2/8	6-4/8	2/8
Circumference Between Second and Third Points	7-3/8	7-4/8	1/8
Circumference Between Third and Fourth Points	7-0/8	6-7/8	1/8
Totals	**93-5/8**	**95-5/8**	**3-2/8**

Exact Location of Kill:	Spread:	20-1/8	
Wisconsin	Column 1:	93-5/8	Final
Taken by:	Column 2:	95-5/8	Score:
James Jordan on Nov. 20, 1914	**Subtotal:**	**209-3/8**	
Measured by:	minus Column 4:	3-2/8	**206-1/8**
George Church Jr. on Feb. 28, 1966	minus Abnormal:	none	

The Hanson Buck: The Final Score

Final Score: 213-5/8

The Stats:

Scorable Points: 14
Right Antler 8
Left Antler 6
Inside Spread: 27-2/8

Abnormal Points: 3-1/8
Right Antler 1-2/8, 1-7/8
Greatest Spread: 29-0/8
Tip-to-Tip Spread: 24-3/8

Area	Right	Left	Difference
Length of Main Beam	28-4/8	28-4/8	
Length of First Point	6-5/8	6-0/8	5/8
Length of Second Point	12-4/8	13-1/8	5/8
Length of Third Point	13-6/8	14-0/8	2/8
Length of Fourth Point	11-4/8	11-5/8	1/8
Length of Fifth Point	5-0/8	7-0/8	2-0/8
Circumference Between Burr and First Point	4-6/8	5-0/8	2/8
Circumference Between First and Second Points	4-2/8	4-2/8	
Circumference Between Second and Third Points	4-3/8	4-2/8	1/8
Circumference Between Third and Fourth Points	4-2/8	4-2/8	
Totals	**95-4/8**	**98-0/8**	**7-1/8**

Exact Location of Kill:
Seven miles north of Biggar,
Saskatchewan, Canada
Taken by: Milo Hanson , 11/23/93.
Measured by: Boone & Crockett
scoring panels.

Spread:	27-2/8
Column 1:	95-4/8
Column 2:	98-0/8
Subtotal:	**220-6/8**
minus Column 4:	7-1/8
minus Abnormal:	3-1/8

Final Score:

213-5/8

The Jordan Buck, which stood as the top whitetail for many years, features massive antlers and great symmetry.

The Hanson Buck, our new world record, features incredible tine lengths, symmetry and spread.

Milo's smile says it all: His buck, the world record typical white-tailed deer, scored 213-5/8, 7-1/2 inches greater than the previous record, the Jordan Buck.

Epilogue

Shooting the Hanson Buck has made my hunting more enjoyable. If I ever felt pressure before to shoot the biggest buck around, it's certainly gone now because I have that buck.

Now I am ready to rest on my laurels, and I have no problem with that. I will never see another deer like the Hanson Buck, and so I can enjoy hunting for what it really is to me: companionship, and the good fortune to be outdoors enjoying and appreciating nature. Our group will still try for big bucks to enter in the local trophy night contests, but none of us will be upset if we don't have an entry.

Some have asked if I worry about someone shooting a bigger buck than mine. I have made up my mind not to worry about it. I have no control over it. Whatever happens will happen. But I still enjoy hearing about big bucks that other people have shot. I like to know the buck's size, who got it, where it was taken, and how it was hunted.

I have a deep interest in trophy whitetails because I know what it takes for antlers to score that high. At one time I was amazed at 170-class bucks. I thought they were rare monsters, but now I believe truly rare, huge bucks have to score more than 200.

What has changed since I shot the Hanson Buck? For one, many people now recognize me in our community and when I travel. My picture with the Hanson Buck has been published so often that many strangers have stopped to congratulate me or to talk deer hunting. I've also noticed a significant awareness of white-tailed deer and trophy whitetails in our community.

Another thing that has changed is my own hunting. I've learned a lot lately about rattling antlers and deer calls. Ian McMurchy is fascinated with calls, scents and camouflage, and has shared his knowledge with me. These items have added another dimension to my hunting. Until Ian came along, I was not accustomed to coaxing in unsuspecting deer, or trying to get closer to them.

I'm also ready for some new forms of hunting. I intend to try hunting bears in the future, including black bears with my muzzle-loading rifle. I have never hunted bears before, even though northern Saskatchewan is famous for them.

Without a doubt, the Hanson Buck, and the financial windfall it provided, have given my life a huge boost and changed it dramatically. Having the additional income has even given me more confidence in making important decisions for our farm. Farmers in western Canada have little control over the sale of our commodities, and absolutely no control over the biggest production factor — weather. The new income has also meant that I no longer need to seek off-farm employment, which I sometimes did in the past when grain prices were poor.

Probably the most negative aspect of shooting the Hanson Buck has been worrying about how everything affects my wife. Olive has tolerated significant changes in our lifestyle. I am fortunate that she has been able to adjust to the demands placed on our time, privacy and energy. We have weathered some trying times as we grappled with instant fame and celebrity status.

In brief, Olive gives me the strength to do the things I find difficult. I am a lucky man.